August 18, 1980.

"Justice or Revolution contains 189 pages and there isn't a wasted word in it. Never in my life have I ever given the slightest thought to having a woman as president of the United States, but...I would be glad to have Leslie Snyder in the White House. She would take us back to the fundamentals laid down in the Constitution by the Founding Fathers...She would not let the government regulate our lives...

I hope that these brief passages will lead you to buy the book...You will be richly rewarded.
I will close with the wish that every member of Congress would read this book and that it would be made required reading in every course in government in every college and university in the land. It would go far to make our beloved country stronger and happier." Henry R. Johnston, "Brain Fare," The *Beaches Leader,* The Jacksonville Beaches, Florida, January 10, 1980.

WHY GOLD?
The One Sure Cure for Inflation and Economic Tyranny

By

LESLIE SNYDER BATES

An Exposition-University Book

EXPOSITION PRESS NEW YORK

authorHOUSE®

AuthorHouse™
1663 Liberty Drive, Suite 200
Bloomington, IN 47403
www.authorhouse.com
Phone: 1-800-839-8640

First published by AuthorHouse 3/30/2010

ISBN: 978-1-4490-3821-2 (e)
ISBN: 978-1-4490-3819-9 (sc)
ISBN: 978-1-4490-3820-5 (hc)

Printed in the United States of America
Bloomington, Indiana

This book is printed on acid-free paper.

First Edition

Library of Congress Catalog Card Number: 73-92853

ISBN 0-682-47884-9

To Dale Bates,
who makes everything possible, even love

Excerpts from Leslie Snyder Bates' Books

WHY GOLD?

"*Why Gold?*" is a refreshing book. It is also the best publication for neophytes in monetary economics on American bookshelves. It should be in every American home...
Authoress Leslie Snyder has done a credible job of research, going far back into antiquity for source material...
Leslie Snyder is well grounded in economics and in the efficacy of gold. Her book is a gem." Oakley R. Bramble, *Inflation Survival Letter*, published by Human Events, Washington D.C., 1974.

"Miss Snyder has just published a truly remarkable little book which I highly recommend to all NCLG members...This is the perfect book for what we might call the 'gold beginner.' Jim Blanchard, Director of National Committee to Legalize Gold, 1974.

"..Highly readable and easy-to-understand book..." Jeffrey St. John, Copley News Service, *The Register*, Orange County, California, April 15, 1974.

"*Why Gold?*" is a newly published book whose time has come. In the middle of today's economic chaos, Leslie Snyder goes right to the heart of the trouble—INFLATION.
...Miss Snyder goes after inflation with remarkable knowledge and skill... It is highly recommended." *American Gold News,* Ione, California, April, 1974.

"It is a thorough and understandable study, which gets to the heart of the economic problem, states it concisely and well, and is highly readable." R. J. Rushdoony of Chalcedon

"I recommend Leslie Snyder's new book entitled *"Why Gold?"*...It is fascinating!" Andre Levie

"Your book is excellent and I particularly appreciated your philosophy and research on the early days of our nation and freedom...I also especially admired your summation of the role of gold in the ancient world. Such a small book, so much research! It should be entitled, 'Gold and You in a Nutshell.' " C. Austin Barker, V.P., Consulting Economist, Hornblower & Weeks, Hemphill, Noyes.

GOLD & BLACK GOLD

"Her book...provides a set of economic prescriptions in a lucid style which even the Founders of the Republic would warmly endorse.
Someone should give President Ford, every member of his Cabinet and member of the new Congress a copy of Leslie Snyder's *"Gold and Black Gold."* In less than 150 pages she provides a brilliant blueprint for getting us out of the economic mess created by government in the last four decades." Jeffrey St. John, *Today's Sunbeam,* Washington, January 6, 1975.

"The author has honed her talent for explaining difficult economic ideas to the lay reader. This book cuts her niche as a writer. Her understanding is deeper, her ideas more original, her logic clear, her writing forceful. For this kind of explanatory writing there should always be a market..." *Financial Book Digest*

"Snyder's book is well worth its price, and highly recommended for both its cool-headed reasoning and its wealth of practical information." Petr Beckmann, *Inflation Survival Letter,* April 7, 1975.

"Leslie Snyder has an uncommon knowledge and expertise in both economics and monetary matters, and she writes well...written by a lady who is compiling a fantastic batting average for excellency." Oakley R. Bramble, *Laissez Faire Review,* Jan.-Feb. 1975.

JUSTICE OR REVOLUTION

"Miss Snyder points out ...the 1961 version (of *Webster's*) added a new meaning to the word (justice), that of 'lawfulness,' which is deceitful and misleading. Law should be based on justice, the author points out; justice is not based on law.
It would be a good textbook for young people, and a good primer on civics and political science for anyone...
The crux of the problem, she says, is that the American people do not expect high moral standards in government; hence, we do not get them.

Justice or Revolution shows the reader how far we have gone along the road to tyranny. But it also shows us how we can save our republic, freedom and justice." Peter Stahl, *SPOTLIGHT*, Liberty Library, Washington, D.C.,

CONTENTS

PREFACE

When asked what type of government the Founding Fathers had created, Benjamin Franklin answered, "A republic, if you can keep it." We are in the last throes of that republic. Democracy has been replacing the republic and is yielding to socialism. The main battle of the 19th century was a central bank because control of the money supply was the seat of power. Alexander Hamilton fought for a strong central government and a strong central bank, which existed on and off throughout the 1900s, finally gaining permanence in 1913 with the Federal Reserve Act.

That shifted the power from the individual to government. The 20th century is known for its wars which were made possible by the Federal Reserve. The power was now in the hands of the few to enrich themselves at the expense of the many. When President Nixon closed the gold window in 1971, the world went on a fiat dollar standard. The fiat dollar removed any restraint on the central bank, the Fed. The bubble burst in 2007. Decades of inflation and credit expansion came to an end. The Fed came to the rescue of those caught in the meltdown. Loaning money and credit in prodigious amounts, it has spent over $2 trillion to cover the losses created by its own irresponsible management.

The Fed doesn't have any money; it creates it out of thin air and charges the debt to us. The country is bankrupt—morally as well as economically. Every check on Congress and the Fed has been circumvented. Only the gold standard can secure our money, property and freedom.

I wrote *Why Gold?* 35 years ago to help dispel the ignorance about the nature of coin, credit and circulation. Evidently, I didn't succeed. Ignorance about money is nearly universal. In the past 35 years our government has been spending money like a drunken sailor who never sobers up. Government has been financing wars on crime, drugs, teen pregnancies, poverty; financing domestic social and welfare programs; policing the world, and exporting our inflation until foreign countries are flooded with dollars. Government uses its "domestic and international wars" to increase its size and power, thereby limiting our freedom in the process.

When *Why Gold?* was written in 1973, Americans weren't legally allowed to own gold. Gold ownership was legalized on December 31, 1974 by an act of

Congress. But we are still ignorant of the nature of our money, capitalism and property rights. This book will dispel that ignorance, allowing Americans to stand up against big government and demand that their rights be respected and protected. The most important right is a sound monetary system with sound money. Only gold can deliver that. After reading the book, I think you will agree.

Since 1945 there have been only two presidents with a vision of the greatness of the United States: John F. Kennedy and Ronald Reagan. The other presidents, by not seeing that America is the last bastion of freedom, have been pandering to foreign governments while destroying our rights.

We are witnessing capitalism's finest hour as we are in the final stages before dissolving into government control, whether it is fascism, dictatorship, or socialism, brought about by the spread of fear, greed and dishonesty in government. This is tyranny!

One example of political tyranny: The Obama administration is trying to renegotiate the Kyoto Protocol, which would give away American sovereignty. We are losing our moral authority. "People who expect to retain the benefits of sovereignty—benefits like defense and protection of rights—without constitutional discipline, or without retaining responsibility for their own legal system, are ...hanging a lot on...some kind of witchcraft." (*Imprimis*, July/August 2009.)

Another example of the spread of power-hungry government is gun control, which benefits governments' intent on controlling its citizens. This is political tyranny! Only criminals benefit from gun controls when honest citizens cannot defend themselves. What kind of government would want to leave its citizens defenseless? When Hitler took over his first step was gun registration; his second, gun confiscation. The rest is history.

A third example is of economic tyranny where government is making deals with big pharmaceuticals. This is a typical example of government in bed with big business, and why separating government from the economy is vital to the preservation of individual freedom. Lying is normal for both parties, the cost of drugs are higher to ensure higher profits, and a huge advertising campaign is being paid for by big pharma to push nationalized healthcare. The government must believe it can sell us anything if pushed long and hard enough.

The headline in Dr. Mercola's 9/12/2009 newsletter is "Huge Giveaways in White House Deal with Big Pharma." A memo reveals that the White House and the pharmaceutical lobby secretly agreed to precisely the sort of wide-ranging deal that both parties have been denying.

While representatives from both the White House and PhRMA have denied that the above deal took place, both the *New York Times* and the *Los Angeles Times* have reported otherwise. The behind-the-scenes deal negotiated by the Senate Finance Committee in June essentially limits drug companies' share of costs of national health care reform to a total of $80 billion over 10 years.

Meanwhile, the White House agreed to oppose any congressional efforts to use the government's leverage to bargain for lower drug prices or import drugs from Canada or Europe. Nearly everyone recognizes that this type of "behind-closed-doors" agreement gives the drug companies a secure seat at the table on Capitol Hill… PhRMA, the drug companies' trade association, is even going to help underwrite a $150 million television ad campaign supporting new health care legislation!

A fourth example of political/economic tyranny is the current healthcare crisis, which is a result of W.W. II government wage controls and tax incentives (See Chapter 7), and for-profit hospitals taken over by government. ("American Healthcare Fascialism," by Thomas J. DiLorenzo, 10/23/2009, www.mises.org).

Example number five is, the Association of Community Organizations for Reforms Now (ACORN), which was formed in 1994. It has received $53 million in direct federal funding and likely more through states and localities that receive federal block grants. According to the U.S. Census Bureau, "It is evident that ACORN is incapable of using federal funds in a manner that is consistent with the law…ACORN should not receive another penny of American taxpayers' money." Letters to President Obama, including one from the IRS, are calling for him to sever all ties to ACORN, as it is under criminal investigation (www.politico.com,9/15/2009).

Government uses fear and lies to control and manipulate us to take away our rights. Our government was set up by a freedom loving people, but it's run by the power hungry who are enslaving us in the name of safety and security.

We are handcuffing the wrong people. We need handcuffs on government and we need them now. Take away their funding and government backs off. Take away the Fed, the central bank, and the funding dries up. Adopt the gold standard and the Fed disappears, and along with it inflation and big government including all the evils it is creating. Freedom is the answer. Now is the time to wrest control and restore our rights guaranteed in the Constitution.

In the fall of 2007 while gold went from $640 an ounce in the summer to $840 an ounce within a few months, my son, Joey, called me from college about some financial crisis in the news. I don't remember the issue, but I do remember how frustrated he sounded that he couldn't figure out what was happening. He was graduating from college soon with a major in Information Technology and a minor in business finance and had taken several economic and business classes, yet he hadn't been taught how they applied to everyday situations. He called me for an explanation, which I gave him in a few words. His frustration was over the convoluted Keynesian economics taught in college, which I had never been brainwashed with. He suggested that I reprint *Why Gold?* Never having taken modern macro and micro economic courses, I don't know what they teach. What I do know is that they haven't taught that 2 + 2 = 4, and paper + ink doesn't = money, and paper + ink x printing press to the 10th or 100th power doesn't = wealth. Modern Keynesian economics has successfully obfuscated the nature of money, capitalism and property rights.

This summer I agreed to reprint the book. Joey has helped me extensively in revising and editing the book. I am grateful for his excellent research, grammar and computer skills. I couldn't have done it without him.

I am also indebted to Rep. Ron Paul for his two books, *The Case for Gold* and *End The Fed* for their history of how our government systematically subverted and destroyed the gold standard and how the Federal Reserve has caused inflation and the current economic meltdown. The winners of the boom and bust cycles are big bankers, big government, the military/industrial complex, big pharmaceuticals, big business and the special interest friends of these groups. The losers are the honest and hard working individuals, small businesses, the retirees, savers for education or retirement purposes, and all who love freedom.

The good news is Ron Paul has introduced three bills to stop this attack on our lives and liberties, HR 3394, The Health Information Act to inhibit the FTC; HR 3395 The Health Freedom Act to remove the unconstitutional power of the FDA; HR 3396 The Congressional Responsibility and Accountability Act to prohibit 90% of the legislation being enacted indirectly by agencies rather than Congress (www.healthfreedomalliance.com, 8/13/09). Ron Paul is warning of impending danger. He is fighting for our freedom against galloping government encroachment. His landmark legislation to audit the Fed, HR 1207 and S 604, is gaining momentum in Congress. Let your representatives know you expect them to support Rep. Paul's bills. In fact, demand they vote to protect you and the country or vote them out.

More good news: 28 states now have introduced legislation asserting state sovereignty "partly in response to the conditions" under the Bush-Obama "stimulus" bills that vastly increased the tyranny of the central regime in Washington, according to *The Christian Science Monitor*. Four of the resolutions have passed, in Idaho, South Dakota, Oklahoma, and South Carolina. Two have been rejected, in New Hampshire and Arkansas. 22 are still pending (www.johnseilersblogs.com). Is your state one of them? Here's where you can do some good.

What we are witnessing in Washington may be business as usual and politically correct. But this behavior is economically wrong, immoral and unconstitutional. We are witnessing how easy access to federal money totally corrupts. We are witnessing the moral breakdown of society. All of these examples are predictable results of government interference in our lives. Unless *we the people* do something about it, we will suffer dire consequences. As Jefferson said, "An elective despotism is not the government I voted for." NOW is the time for Americans to take a stand and demand Congress try FREEDOM for a change!

Kennewick, Washington   Leslie Snyder Bates
September 29, 2009

INTRODUCTION

This speech has been attributed to John Adams, the second President of the United States of America, in his fight for American independence.

> Sink or swim, live or die, survive or perish, I give my hand and my heart to this vote . . . Sir, I know the uncertainty of human affairs, but I see, I see clearly, through this day's business. You and I, indeed, may rue it. We may not live to see the time when this Declaration shall be made good . . . But whatever may be our fate, be assured, be assured, that this Declaration will stand . . .
>
> Sir, before God, I believe the hour is come. My judgment approves this measure, and my whole heart is in it. All that I have, and all that I am, and all that I hope in this life, I am now ready here to stake upon it; and I leave off as I began, that live or die, survive or perish, I am for the Declaration. It is my living sentiment, and by the blessing of God it shall be my dying sentiment: independence now, and INDEPENDENCE FOREVER.

Independence! That is why we fought the American Revolution; that is why fifty-six men pledged their lives and their fortunes. Blood was shed, lives lost, and property destroyed. All for the cause of freedom and independence. Independence! This is the essence of being an American.

No group of men ever understood the importance of independence more than our Founding Fathers. They knew the history of the rise and fall of great nations so well they founded this new country squarely and firmly on the Gold Standard.

The Gold Standard embodies the principles of monetary freedom and independence. The issue of hard money (the gold standard) versus paper money was the most important issue of the post-Revolutionary era. In fact, the Gold Standard issue has raged from the time of the Revolution to the present.

The four words "not worth a Continental" recall the paper money which caused the runaway inflation that very nearly destroyed the American Revolution. And as a result of that turbulent and devastating runaway inflation, the framers of the Constitution made only gold and silver lawful tender in payment of debts.

During the Civil War, seventy-five years later, Congress enacted a legal tender law, which again forced Americans to accept paper money, and the country, entered another inflationary era. Thirteen years later, in 1875, by an act of Congress, hard money payments were resumed.

Fifty-eight years later by Executive Order of April 5, 1933, Franklin D. Roosevelt prohibited hard money—gold coins, gold bullion, and gold certificates from the recognized and customary channels of trade and required same to be delivered to member banks of the Federal Reserve System.

This amounted to government confiscation of private property. Never before in American history had Americans been prohibited from owning gold. During the Revolution hard money became scarce because of the abundance of paper money. During the Civil War the Western states, especially California, used hard money for trade. But gold has always been freely owned.

The reason why the Gold Standard issue has raged for the greater part of two centuries is simply that the majority of Americans do not understand it. But the importance of the Gold Standard cannot be over-emphasized. It is crucial for the maintenance and improvement of our high standard of living and freedom.

During the 146 years of monetary freedom, from 1787 to 1933, America grew and prospered. Capitalism spread from country to country. The standard of living throughout the industrialized world rose to unprecedented heights. But more important was the fact that the price level of all goods and services during this same time period remained stable. The reasons for this remarkable rate of stable growth were clear: the capitalistic productive system and the stable dollar, which was "as good as gold."

Since 1933, however, Americans have been prohibited from owning gold. This ill-advised action is producing today its predictable results—runaway inflation, oppressive taxation, chronic unemployment, the growth of big government, disrespect for life and property, lack of patriotism, and moral disintegration.

It seems that ignorance about the nature of money has existed in America since the Revolution. In 1829, John Quincy Adams, son of John

Adams and sixth President of the United States, observed that "all the perplexities, confusion and distress in America arise, not from defects in their constitution or confederation, not from want of honor or virtue, so much as from downright ignorance of the nature of coin, credit, and circulation."

History, it seems, has not only proved John Quincy Adams correct, but it appears as though history is repeating itself.

In the two hundred years since American independence, the United States has made the round trip, from inflation and oppressive taxation to monetary freedom, and today we are back to inflation and oppressive taxation. (Must we fight another revolution before we win back our birthright—monetary freedom?)

There must be a renaissance in monetary thinking if the United States is to break out of the monetary whirlpool in which it is sinking. If we want to maintain our high standard of living for which we have worked so long and so hard, we must return to the stability, safety and justice of the Gold Standard.

This course of thinking is contrary to the popular trend. But when the Gold Standard was supreme and undefeatable, monetary freedom and sanity reigned.

The purpose of this book, therefore, is to dispel the ignorance surrounding the nature of coin, credit, and circulation. It shows how to stop inflation and its destructive results, and how to return to monetary freedom and sanity—the Gold Standard.

Oxnard, California   Leslie Snyder
September 17, 1973

PART I

MAN'S RIGHTS AND GOLD

1

THE DECLARATION OF INDEPENDENCE

In 1776, fifty-six men joined together to declare the independence of man. This was the first time in history man had declared he possessed certain "unalienable rights." Those fifty-six men declared: "We hold these truths to be self-evident; that all men are created equal; that they are endowed by their creator with certain unalienable rights; that among these are life, liberty, and the pursuit of happiness . . ." The self-evident truths which the fifty-six Founding Fathers proclaimed, were man's right to live by reason, to choose the purpose of his happiness, and to keep the fruits of his labor. The crucial principle that the Founding Fathers discovered was that man's happiness lay with man, the individual—that man is an end in himself—not the means to the ends of others. These men produced the greatest document the world had ever seen. They produced the American Declaration of Independence.

Thomas Jefferson, author of the Declaration, said the purpose of the Declaration is "to place before mankind the common sense of the subject" and to make this document "an expression of the American mind."

The Declaration, as "an expression of the American mind," concisely states man's rights and defines the purpose and nature of government. It declares:

> . . . that to secure these rights, governments are instituted among men, deriving their just powers from the consent of the governed; that whenever any form of government becomes destructive to these ends, it is the right of the people to alter or to abolish it, and to institute new government, laying its foundation on such principles, and organizing its powers in such form, as to them shall seem most likely to effect their safety and happiness . . . when a long train of abuses and usurpations pursuing invariably the same object, evinces a design to reduce them under absolute despotism,

it is their right, it is their duty, to throw off such government and to provide new guards for their future security.

The Declaration also declares that "... all experience hath shown that mankind is more disposed to suffer while evils are sufferable, than to right themselves by abolishing the forms to which they are accustomed." Jefferson's observation was correct. It took 6,000 years of agonizing history before the people cried: "Enough! Enough of the divine right of kings; enough of inquisitions, economic planners, the tyranny of the mob, of bureaucratic whim and of bureaucratic czars!"

The American colonists rebelled at the idea of being the means by which King George III ruled their lives. They rebelled at the idea of "taxation without representation," that they should be taxed to support British troops they never requested nor wanted, which were to be garrisoned in the colonies. They rebelled at the British Navigation Acts, the Stamp Act, the Townshend Acts, and the Intolerable Acts which severely interfered with their trade.

In every stage of these oppressions the colonists petitioned for redress. But their petitions were answered only by repeated injury.

Emotions were running high. It would not have taken much to bring a showdown between the colonists and the garrisoned British troops. The colonists were already fired up by Patrick Henry's "Give Me Liberty or Give Me Death" speech. And when Paul Revere warned them of oncoming British troops, the colonists readied themselves. They foiled the attempted arrest of Samuel Adams and John Hancock. Interference in the colonists' lives culminated in 1776 at Lexington and Concord, when the first shots of the American Revolution were fired.

By 1776, the fifty-six Founding Fathers realized that there was to be no liberty, freedom or justice under British rule. They were ready to take a stand—to dissolve all political connection between them and the State of Great Britain. On July 4, 1776, standing tall, straight, and unwavering, they solemnly published and declared, "that these United Colonies are, and of right ought to be, free and independent States; that they are absolved from all allegiance to the British Crown . . . And for the support of this declaration . . . we mutually pledge to each other our lives, our fortunes, and our sacred honor."

The price for freedom and independence came very high. It cost some of the Founding Fathers their lives and their fortunes: Five signers were captured by the British as traitors. Twelve had their homes ransacked and burned. Two lost their sons in the Continental Army. Another had two sons captured. Nine of the fifty-six signers fought and died from wounds or the hardships of the American Revolution. But the honor of all fifty-six men survived unscathed, to be remembered with a feeling of pride by all future Americans.

These stories are typical of those who risked everything to sign the Declaration. They were not wild-eyed, rabble-rousing ruffians. They were heroes, men larger than life, who distinguished themselves by forethought and bravery. Twenty-five men were lawyers or jurists. Eleven were merchants. Nine were farmers or large plantation owners. They were men of means and education. They had security, but they valued liberty more. They signed the Declaration of Independence knowing full well that the penalty could be death if they were captured.[1]

"There is a price tag on human liberty," said James Monroe. "That price is being free men. Payment of this price is a personal matter with each of us." Benjamin Franklin summed it up when he said, "They that can give up essential liberty to obtain a little temporary safety, deserve neither liberty nor safety." No, freedom is not free. The price is very high indeed.

To secure the rights for which the revolutionists fought and died, the Founding Fathers produced another great document—The Constitution of the United States of America. William Pitt said, "It will be the wonder and admiration of all future generations and the model of all future constitutions." The English statesman William Gladstone described it as "the most perfect work ever struck off at a given point in time, by the brain and purpose of man."

The Founding Fathers took much care to make sure that the essence of the Constitution was clear, that government should have limited power, because the Founding Fathers were familiar with history and had a deep suspicion of all governments. They believed that one of the great threats to a man's life, liberty and property had always been the government under which he lived. They believed that all governments would, under the excuse of "taking care" of the people, actually enslave the people. In the words of George Washington, "Government is not reason, it is not eloquence; it is force. Like fire, which if it is not controlled, will destroy you." Thomas Jefferson said, "That Government is best which governs least."

Based on their deep suspicion of governments, the Founding Fathers intentionally subordinated government to the individual. The individual can do anything he wishes, except that which infringes upon another individual's rights; government can do only that which the Constitution allows it to do.

The Founding Fathers knew that government's actions must be limited because it holds a monopoly over force. Since only by force can man's rights be abrogated, they purposely wrote the Constitution to limit government which will protect man's rights. *The protection of man's rights from force is the only moral function of government.* Thus, the purpose of the armed forces is to protect man from foreign invasion, the police force from criminals, and the court system from fraud—to protect and enforce contracts which are a prerequisite in a higher form of civilization.

Constitutionalism is the only moral government because it is based on and limited by fundamental laws which protect individual rights. Individual rights start with the right to one's life—the basic and essential right, which makes all other rights possible. The right to one's property and the right to keep the fruits of one's labor implement the right to one's life because they are the means by which one sustains his life and can pursue his happiness.

The alternative to property rights, or no property rights, is slavery. It is either-or. This is the right to take action, not the right or the entitlement to an object. There is no guarantee that a man will earn any property, only the guarantee that he will own it if he earns it. There can be no right to the fruits of the labor of others, because this means those others are deprived of their own rights and condemned to slave labor. There can be no such thing as the right to enslave or the right to destroy rights.

So man will know what his rights are the Constitution provides him with objective, well-defined laws.

The opposite of limited constitutional government is unlimited government, or socialism, statism, communism, Fascism, Marxism, and totalitarianism. Under socialism man's inalienable rights, are not respected. Government has the power to subject the people to absolute rule. What man creates, government owns. There are no property rights.

The third type of government, or no government, is anarchy, where no moral standards, rights, or objective laws are recognized.

Constitutional government is designed to protect man's inalienable rights from government--force, coercion, and interference. This is the meaning of political freedom. It is the only valid justification of a government. The Bill of Rights was designed to declare explicitly that individual rights supersede any public or social power by further limiting the power of government. It reinforced man's individual supremacy over government and society. It was designed by the American people, who had been trained for generations to be jealous and protective of their freedoms.

At the close of the Constitutional Convention, Benjamin Franklin was asked, "What is the kind and form of our government?" He answered, "A Republic—if you can keep it!"

The Founding Fathers never faltered in their conviction that it was a republic they cherished, not a democracy. As Alexander Hamilton said, "We are a Republican Government. Real liberty is never found in despotism or in the extremes of Democracy." The dangers of democracy were also well understood by James Madison, who said, "Democracies have ever been found incompatible with personal security, or the rights of property; and have in general been as short in their lives as they have been violent in their deaths."

The supreme spokesman for liberty in American colonial life was Thomas Jefferson. Looking ahead to future generations he wondered: "Yes, we did produce a near perfect Republic, but will they keep it, or will they in the enjoyment of plenty, lose the memory of freedom? Material abundance without character is the surest way to destruction."

Thomas Jefferson was right. Today the federal government is destroying individual rights and freedom. The reason is that Americans lack integrity, which is reflected in their elected representatives. Americans are choosing a false sense of security over freedom. They have material abundance without character.

Although our inalienable rights were declared in 1776 and established in 1787, their philosophic and economic principles have yet to be understood by the large majority of Americans. Ignorance is not bliss; it is dangerous. Since America has deviated from the principles of the Constitution by allowing government to regulate most aspects of life especially the economy, we are faced with inflation, confiscation, taxation and recessions.

The Founding Fathers had suffered from oppressive taxation and inflation and fought to free themselves from their unjust and injurious consequences. They understood tyranny begins with encroachment on private property. So they conceived of a nation where men were free to keep what they earned, where no oppressive taxation robbed them of their earnings, and no inflation embezzled their hard-earned savings. Their idea of freedom meant absolute and total freedom, not only from political tyranny, but also from economic tyranny.

They were wise as well as brave. They fought the Revolution to free themselves from political and economic tyranny by sacrificing the present for the future, a feat few men can claim. To secure their property from future government encroachment, they produced the Declaration of Independence and the Constitution, with a Bill of Rights. To further secure their property and liberty as best they could, they made *only* gold and silver lawful money.

In fact, gold and silver money was just as important to the Founding Fathers as all their other rights. Gold and silver money was incorporated into Article I, Sections 8 and 10 of the Constitution before the Bill of Rights was written. Only gold and silver money was acceptable to them because it secured their economic freedom (their property and wealth), which, in turn, secured their political freedom. And economic freedom requires monetary freedom and a stable currency made of hard (gold and silver) money.

The next two chapters explain the truths that were implicit in the Declaration's self-evident truths that man has a right to life, liberty, and pursuit of happiness.

The remaining chapters explain what should have been explicit in the Constitution, that to secure the inalienable rights of Americans (and to rid the country of the lethal consequences of government regulations and government created inflation), two requirements must exist in society. The first requirement is a proper economic system, which is Capitalism. The second requirement is a proper monetary system based on gold.

2

THE FOUNDING FATHERS' PHILOSOPHY

The self-evident truths to which the Declaration and the Constitution refer are based on a philosophy of giving life the highest value—man's life.

Man, unlike the animal, has the conscious ability to decide whether or not to live. An animal instinctively hunts for his food—his only basic need. Man's basic needs—food, clothing, and shelter—must first be produced before consumed. Their production is a lifetime endeavor. To produce them, man must think. And to think efficiently, man must have a philosophy.

The philosophy of the Founding Fathers is based on individual rights. It enables man to decide how to produce his basic needs efficiently, how to keep the fruits of his labor. It allows man to understand and protect his rights.

The Founding Fathers were well educated in philosophy. They were mostly second-generation Americans, schooled in individual rights and profoundly dedicated to preserving the rights of free men. They were raised with a deep respect for science and the "natural law." Their basic philosophical principles of life were founded by the seventeenth-century philosopher John Locke.

Those principles were based on a philosophy which strived to understand reality and the laws of nature. Some key ideas of political thought at the time of the Constitutional Convention were: Man's rights flow from nature—they're natural, inalienable and essential to meaningful existence. The greatest rights were life (self-preservation), liberty, property (to use and dispose of the fruits of one's labor), and happiness. A good society existed where the purpose of government was to recognize and protect these natural rights. The best form of government was republican—representative and responsible. One of the most important and essential ideas was that the people always retain the right of resistance against the government, as a last refuge.[1] Also, see the Declaration for "their duty to throw off such government."

In addition to a strong respect for reality and the search for truth, they respected man's mind, the reasoning faculty that enables him to grasp reality. They understood that reason is man's fundamental tool of survival.

Thomas Jefferson understood the tremendous reasoning power of the mind. He believed the meaning of the phrase "pursuit of happiness" was about achieving a balanced life—the harmony of mind, body and spirit, of thought and action, with a resulting serenity and sense of well-being. His adherence to reason over force was exhibited through his admiration of the Constitution, which he conveyed in a letter to David Humphreys on March 18, 1789:

> The example of changing a constitution by assembling the wise men of the state, instead of assembling armies, will be worth as much to the world as the former examples we had given them. The constitution, too, which was the result of our deliberation, is unquestionably the wisest ever yet presented to men.

Men such as Thomas Jefferson, George Washington, James Madison, John Adams, and Benjamin Franklin, were men of principles. They were statesmen. It was their confidence in man's mind, his rationality which forms the basis of the Constitution and the concept of man's inalienable right to life. Because the Founding Fathers believed man was good—a value unto himself—they demanded his freedom, so man could earn his living as he saw fit.

They believed man possessed "free will." He was able to think, to know right from wrong, and thus able to deal successfully with reality. When they proclaimed that man, the individual, superseded government, they threw off the government's control of men over men; they discovered political and economic freedom! As an unprecedented phenomenon in history, the Founding Fathers were not only thinkers but also men of action! Their benevolent philosophy and will to do right based on inalienable, natural rights—unchanging principles—over two hundred years ago, allow Americans to enjoy their constitutional freedoms today.

Since the concept of rights is vital to man's survival, the definition of the word "rights" should be clearly understood. A "right" is a moral principle that defines and sanctions a man's freedom of action in society. The fundamental right that makes all other rights possible is the right to one's life. This is the right to take the action that will sustain and further one's life. The nature and essence of man demands this right. This is freedom of action—to be free from force and coercion by other men, groups of men, or government. Therefore, a right sanctions an action—freedom for every individual to think, judge, and act by his own voluntary, uncoerced choice.

The concept of individual rights is so prodigious a feat of political thinking that few men grasp it fully—and two hundred years have not been enough for other countries to understand and implement it. But men owe their lives to this concept. The concept of individual rights has made it possible for people to bring into existence everything anyone ever did or ever will produce, achieve, or experience.

The concept of individual rights manifests itself in the right to property, the only means of implementing the right to life. Property rights allow man to take the actions that are required to sustain his life. By knowing he can keep what he earns, man can plan long-term. This is important to man because the path to prosperity differs than that of the animal which is based on survival of the moment. Some projection of the future is a necessity of man's survival. Rights to life and property are inalienable rights. To alienate man from these rights is to alienate him from his life.

Political and economic freedom means the right to life and property. Political freedom requires economic freedom—separating the state from the economy. The only moral economic system is capitalism—the private ownership of the means of production. It means a totally unregulated and uncontrolled economy with a free exchange of goods and services. Laissez-faire capitalism requires the freedom to think and the right to property—the translation of one's thoughts into action.

When one grasps the principles of the American philosophy of individual rights, one can understand the concepts required by a free society. One can understand the importance of free trade, the right to the fruits of one's labor and the destructive results from government interference in either. One can grasp that political and economic freedom require the right to property —especially the individual right to own, trade and use gold.

Ask any socialist about gold—he knows it must be destroyed as a standard of value in order to give government ultimate control over economic freedom. Americans are not very familiar with the importance gold serves in an economy free of government control. They must learn that private ownership of gold and the use of a freely circulating gold-backed currency, an inalienable right, can guard their life, liberty, and pursuit of happiness. The Founding Fathers' philosophy explains the importance of gold. In fact, the right to own and use gold is the difference between freedom and slavery.

3

MAN WORKS FOR PROFIT AND PLEASURE

Man's basic needs must be produced before they can be consumed. Production is the application of reason to the problem of survival. Life is a process of self-generating and self-sustaining action. When man works he is converting his mental and physical energy into products or services that will sustain and enhance his life.

Productive work is one of man's most fundamental areas of pleasure. Through work, man gains a basic sense of control over his life. In controlling his life, he earns his self-confidence—confidence in his mind. The feeling of confidence that comes from knowing one is able to meet and overcome new challenges is pleasurable.

Experiencing pleasure is very important to man. It is a profound psychological need. Through the state of enjoyment, man experiences the value of life, the sense that life is worth living, worth struggling to maintain. Pleasure serves as the emotional fuel to propel him onward to greater achievements.

Pleasure is the reward of successful action and pain is the signal of danger. Pain is the penalty of unsuccessful action and implies the feeling of helplessness. The continuation of pain and suffering will lead to failure, destruction and death.

Since the activity of pursuing and achieving values or goals is the essence of the life-process, happiness or suffering may be regarded as an "incentive system" built into man, a system of reward and punishment, designed to further and protect man's life.[1]

Since man must work to survive and his work can bring immense pleasure, he should choose the career which he thinks will be the most rewarding.

The first choice man must make is between working on a self-sustaining farm or joining the division of labor in society. On the farm his production is limited but self sustaining. In society, if he devotes his effort to a special field, while others do the same, there is an overall greater return on production. The division of labor in society raises everybody's standard of living.

Assuming man is free to choose the career which he thinks and feels he will derive the utmost happiness, and he chooses to live and work in society, certain conditions of society are required in order for him to function efficaciously in the division of labor. The first condition is that man must be allowed to live by reason. He must be free to think, to produce, and to trade without force or coercion. When force is not permitted, discussion, persuasion, and voluntary agreement or disagreement prevails. He must be free to trade with whom he chooses, when he chooses, and for how much he chooses. The market must be free to determine the price of all products and wages. In order for the market to be free, society must be completely free from government interference—separate state and economics.

Where society is free from government interference such tariffs, quotas, regulations and taxes, man can earn from his work the two most important rewards. The first reward is material. The harder a man works the more he produces, bringing more wealth into existence. As man's efficiency increases his profit increases, and the wealthier he becomes. This is the American dream.

The other reward man earns from his work is intangible. It is the emotional pleasure that comes from doing a good job, from being productive and being able to survive. Competence in his work earns man his self-respect. And, together, self-confidence and self-respect earn man his self-esteem, which is a basic psychological need for survival.

A free society attracts men of ambition and productiveness. A free society is a prerequisite to a high standard of living. Only where man is free to choose his life's work, able to advance in his work as far as his ability can take him, and able to retain the material rewards of his labor, can he experience the pleasure he has rightfully earned.

Profit and pleasure are the incentives that drive man onward to greater achievements. There is no better way to retain the value of his created wealth—earnings, savings, and investments—than by receiving payment in gold or gold-backed money. Gold is practically indestructible. The fleeting energy of man can thus be preserved and transformed into enduring gold.

4

WHAT IS MONEY?

All self-supporting men work to convert their mental and physical energy into products or services to produce value for their effort. Since man must produce to survive and money is what he is paid for his labor, it is important to know what money is, and, in particular, what good money is.

In olden days, to a cobbler, plying his craft from a bench under a tree, good money was a gold coin, of relatively pure content. Saved at the end of a day, it was a financial reserve, and his bank was his wife's arms and ankles, which he could encircle with these savings. The bracelets and anklets of coins afforded security against famine, depression, or old age, and might provide the capital whereby he could graduate from the ranks of a street cobbler and acquire his own shop, and progress to affluence, as far as his ambition could take him. But when he could no longer save a piece of gold, but was forced accept instead a piece of paper that if saved could be eaten by termites or destroyed by rain, and in any case, depreciated from month to month, then his hopes for rising in the world were cut off and he became an unhappy prey to unrest and revolutionary plotting.

In essence, money is the means of survival. And good, hard money is the means to freedom, independence, and wealth. Soft, depreciating money is deceitful and leads to poverty, slavery, unrest, and revolution.

Philosophically, money is the material shape of the honest principle to give value for value which fosters trust between men. Man's mind is the root of all the goods and wealth ever produced. Money is a tribute to the glory and accomplishments of man.

Money is the means of survival for free men. To condemn money is to condemn one's survival. To abandon money is to abandon freedom and embrace force and coercion. The man who earns money inherently respects it.

There is only one society, one country that is a "country of money"—the United States of America. Americans have the distinction no other nation can claim; they are the people who created the phrase "to make money." Previously, men had always thought of wealth as a static quantity—to be seized, begged, inherited, shared, looted or obtained as a favor. Americans are the first to understand that wealth has to be first created. Money is made—before it can be expropriated and redistributed—made by the effort of every honest man, each to the extent of his ability.

In modern society, when money ceases to be the medium of exchange by which men deal with one another, only one arbiter remains—the gun. A society run by force and coercion is doomed. To prevent man's destruction, one must grasp the essential principle: *Money is the root of all good.*

In the concrete sense, money is a commodity. It is the most marketable commodity, generally accepted and commonly used. It is acquired with the intention of later trading it. As a commodity, there can be too much or too little of it. If there is too much in circulation, each unit is worth less. If there is too little in circulation, each unit is worth more.

Money is a vehicle for economic calculation. It is the common denominator in all economic transactions. It functions as a medium of exchange. If men were to barter, trade product for product, such as a basket of eggs for a pair of shoes, no money would be required. However, in advanced societies where men specialize in one field, primitive bartering is not practical. Goods and services require a medium of exchange—money. Most goods and services are bought and sold against money—no goods, no use for money. Money means prices—no money, no way to determine prices. Money is worth only what it can buy, its purchasing power.

Money should serve three functions. First, it is a means of payment. Money is used to pay bills, to buy and sell goods and services. Second, it is a standard of value. The values of goods and services are quoted in terms of money. The resulting ratios are prices. Third, it is a store of value. It should retain its value throughout time. Money should always be scarce; when it is not, it becomes a free good, devoid of value.

Good money must meet four requirements. It must be a commodity that possesses intrinsic value. Throughout history many mediums of exchange have been used and have had their shortcomings—cattle died; grain spoiled; human heads went out of vogue; silk ruined; logs awkward; spices spoiled; salt took too much; shells broke; feathers, furs, and whale teeth were not in steady supply.

The second requirement is that the commodity must not be too abundant, rendering it worthless, or too scarce, rendering it unattainable. It must have a steady supply to keep its value constant.

Third, its worth must be easily recognized. It must be durable, portable, divisible and universally accepted. Finally, it must be independent of government decree. It must be accepted by choice. Ludwig von Mises observed, "The government is the only agency that can take a useful commodity like paper, slap some ink on it, and make it totally worthless." Fiat paper money is money of mere tokens which can neither be employed as a useful commodity nor redeemable into something of value. Money independent of government decree would nullify "legal tender" laws. No one should be forced to accept a less desirable commodity as money.

Around 700 B.C., as man emerged from the bartering stage of human life into the commercial stage, gold pellets were gaining acceptance as a medium of exchange in the markets. Since they differed in size, weight and fineness, they were awkward and time-consuming, for all pellets had to be graded for fineness and weighed for value. Perceiving this, Croesus, the clever King of Lydia, invented the coinage of gold.

> With the help of coined gold money, Lydian producers and traders made their nation the foremost commercial success of the ancient world. The secret of that success was the powerful incentive furnished by gold coinage in preserving the fleeting energy of men by transformation into enduring gold. The gold would keep; the perishable products would spoil. Better have gold than spoiling products.[1]

Evolution has eliminated most media of exchange. Gold and silver have endured the test of time. Gold has facilitated trade for thousands of years. Even today, knowledgeable citizens demand their government back their nation's currency with gold, and insist that the citizens be allowed to own gold, as insurance against the government tampering with the currency, impairing its value. As a medium of exchange, gold establishes trust between traders—be they individuals or governments. A lack of gold portends a breakdown in trade. A stable currency is a precondition to the division of labor. When workers are paid their worth in gold or a stable, gold-backed currency, work continues. All receive value for value. The stability of gold allows savings, and savings are the necessary means with which to save and invest for the future.

As a commodity, gold has intrinsic value; it is used for thousands of things—from measurement instrumentation to computers, from curing cancer to rheumatoid arthritis. It even protects astronauts from the blazing heat of the sun. In industry, it is one of the most useful metals. Gold is neither too abundant nor too scarce. Mines produce a steady supply of it. The worth of a gold coin is easily recognizable because its weight and fineness are stamped directly on each coin. Gold coins are practically indestructible; they cannot corrode, rust or tarnish. Gold coins can be easily moved—a little bit goes a long way; they can be carried off in an emergency and are accepted universally. Gold is easily molded into coins of small or large denominations or worked into jewelry. Finally, gold can be easily minted by private mints, independent of government decree. When it is free to trade side by side with government currency, the free market determines the value of each medium of exchange.

There is only one effective way to insure that money retains its value. Ideally, the money supply would expand and contract roughly in proportion to the expansion and contraction of goods and services exchanged *independent* of any arbitrary manipulation by anyone person or government. The money supply automatically adjusts and the general price level remains substantially unchanged. The gold standard is the only system proven to maintain stable prices. Over relatively short periods, it is similar to a fixed money supply, which keeps prices stable and nearly fixed. Over relatively long periods of time, the gold standard system expands and contracts roughly in proportion to the long-term expansion in production, according to the vicissitudes of gold mining. And, most importantly, it is a system in which the volume of the money supply is *independent* of arbitrary manipulation by anyone.

The Founding Fathers appreciated the value of gold and silver money. They fought long and hard to put an end to fiat paper money. To insure the use of gold and silver money by future generations, Article I, Section 8 of the Constitution gives Congress the power "to coin money," not to print it. In addition, Article I, Section 10 states: "No state shall . . . make anything but gold and silver coin a tender in payment of debts." The Founding Fathers understood gold was money and money was gold, the best that could be had. It was one of the most important rights they secured for future generations.

Gold is the ultimate form of money; it is not managed or manipulated. It has no nationality; it is universally trusted and accepted. It is the universal standard for money and store of value. Gold is treasured and honored throughout the world as the supreme standard of value. Whenever fiat paper money falls in disrepute, people seek protection for their wealth and economic freedom in gold. Gold is truly good money—the best form of money. It is out of government's control; it is a refuge for citizens who mistrust politicians; it allows 'financial transactions beyond the reach and manipulation of the government. In the not too distant past, gold was for many the means of escape to freedom. Throughout thousands of years of government propaganda, edicts, and confiscations, nothing has replaced gold; and it is doubtful anything ever will.

5

WHAT IS CAPITALISM?

The gold standard springs eternally from freedom and succumbs to laws and regulations. Its implacable enemy is government in search of revenue. Whereas, individuals produce goods and services in order to earn their living, government expropriates individual income and wealth in order to cover its expenses. Winston Churchill observed that the crime against society is not profit, but loss: "Private industry runs at a profit and uses the profit to expand producing capacity. Government industry runs at a loss and taxes the substance of the people to pay for its inefficiencies . . ."

The government's appetite for revenue is insatiable. It is vital to understand the purpose of the gold standard is to prevent government encroachment on private property. The gold standard works within the economic system. It is part of Capitalism.

> The gold standard is not important as an isolated gadget but only as an integral part of a whole economic system. Just as "managed" paper money goes with a statist and collectivist philosophy, with government "planning," with a coercive economy in which the citizen is always at the mercy of bureaucratic caprice, so the gold standard is an integral part of a free-enterprise economy under which governments respect private property, economize in spending, balance their budgets, keep their promises, and refuse to connive in overexpansion of money or credit...[1]

Since the gold standard is an integral part of the capitalistic system, which promotes political and economic freedom, the study of capitalism is vital to the preservation of a free society.

Capitalism is the private ownership of the means of production. Capitalism is the only economic system that can protect and uphold individual rights. A controlled or managed economy is not based on individual rights, and cannot protect or uphold individual rights. Capitalism is the only moral economic system.

The case of the capitalistic economy versus the managed or planned economy has been on trial for the last two hundred years. It is the choice between the Declaration of Independence and the Communist Manifesto. It is the choice between freedom and slavery. The choice exists; it must be made.

Capitalism is under constant attack in the schools and by pseudo-intellectuals; it is time to give it a fair trial. Understanding and appreciating economics is crucial to the maintenance of a free society. It should be the concern of every American. Nothing can be more important to every intelligent man than economics. His future economic and physical health are at stake. For this purpose the fundamental concepts of capitalism are the subject of this chapter.

Capitalism is the life-blood of a free society. It explains such wonders as: Who came first—the employer or the employee? Who runs the market —the producer or the consumer? Capitalism exposes the truths that have been obfuscated by Keynesian economists, by monetarists, by our federal government and by ignorant news media parroting the deceits. The study of freedom and capitalism is eye-opening and exciting. For the man who never relents in his search for truth, economics, especially capitalism, is dynamic.

In eighteenth-century France the saying "laissez-faire" was the slogan for the champions of liberty. Their purpose was the establishment of the free market. In order to attain this end they advocated the abolition of all laws preventing more industrious and more efficient individuals from outdoing less industrious and less efficient competitors.

Laissez-faire means: Let each individual choose what he wants to do to in the division of labor; let the consumers determine what the entrepreneurs produce. Planning means: Let government alone choose and enforce its rulings by force and coercion. The question that must be decided is one of morality; which is right: Should man plan his own life, or should government plan it for him? It is individual freedom versus government omnipotence. Laissez-faire means: Let man choose how to act; do not force him to yield to a dictator or czar.[2]

Laissez-faire capitalism means a separation of state and economics, a totally unregulated and uncontrolled economy. It is free minds and a free market where trade is based on choice—no force or coercion. The free market is a series of unlimited, voluntary exchanges between individuals for their own mutual benefit. As a result of the free price system, consumers' buying or abstention from buying channels production into the areas in demand by the consumer. The law of supply and demand works efficiently. Capitalism gives the economy sense and society functions orderly.

The essential role of government in a capitalistic society is to defend individual rights by protecting the nation and the marketplace. Every step it takes beyond that role, whether foreign or domestic is a step toward a system of socialism where there is no freedom. In the marketplace, when government interferes or takes certain liberties, it is taking those liberties from individuals out of the marketplace. Government forces the market to respond in a way different than the consumers want. Liberty and freedom are the conditions of man within a contractual society. Within a free market individuals are buyers or sellers by choice. Man works because he wants to be rewarded; he does not submit to compulsory labor nor does he pay tribute. He exchanges goods and services on the same basis. The buyer depends on the seller and the seller on the buyer. This is social cooperation in the division of labor. All receive value. Capitalism insures justice in the marketplace.

A basic requirement for the functioning of capitalism is a sound currency, a stable medium of exchange. When money continually depreciates, long-term contracts and savings become unprofitable. It is important the marketplace choose the best medium of exchange, one that will protect future profits. Free people have historically chosen gold and silver. When contracts are honored in gold, long-term planning and saving is profitable. When workers are paid in gold, silver or gold-backed money, work continues, and the capitalistic system thrives.

Capitalism is the private ownership of the means of production. The function of the entrepreneur is to determine the employment of the factors of production. A capitalist runs the risk of losing his capital; he is also a speculator. A speculator is one who buys something in expectation of it rising in value. Nearly all Americans are speculators because there is no such thing as a risk free investment; there are only varying degrees of risk. The worker is concerned with changes in the labor market. Thus every function is integrated: the entrepreneur earns a profit or suffers a loss; the owners of the means of production (capital goods or land) earn interest; the workers earn wages.[3]

The entrepreneur is the driving force of the market. The direction of the market is the task of the entrepreneur. He controls production. He is at the helm and steers the ship. He is bound to obey unconditionally the captain's orders. The captain is the consumer.[4] The entrepreneur is driven by his own self interest in making profits and in acquiring wealth.

Profit is the key to capitalism. No one will risk his wealth if there is no chance of profit. Profit is the incentive to take risks. No profit means no incentive; this can lead to a shortage of capital and a lack of progress. An economy will stagnate and eventually retrogress without profit. To condemn profits is to encourage losses. The entrepreneur is motivated by profits. Income, wealth, and production are the results of thinking and action—employed by the entrepreneur for his profit and the benefit of society.

Profit not only serves as incentive for entrepreneurs and capitalists, but also allows capital accumulation or savings. Savings is the life-blood of an industrial society. Through investment of savings, new plants and equipment can be created and employed. Efficient plants and equipment yield higher productivity and higher productivity yield a higher the standard of living. The reason why the United States enjoys such a high standard of living is because the amount of invested savings per capita is greater than anywhere else in the world. Capital accumulation of profit is a prerequisite for a high standard of living.

Capitalism increases worker's real wage rates to the extent of reinvested capital. Savings and capital accumulation are an indispensable condition for technological improvement. Technology increases the output per unit of input, yielding higher productivity and a higher standard of living. "A tendency toward higher wage rates is not the cause, but the effect, of technological improvement."[5] The wages of workers in capitalistic countries far exceed those of non-capitalistic countries.

A high standard of living is the result of the production of more goods. Wealth is goods, something with intrinsic value, not paper money. One cannot buy prosperity with paper money; it must be created, i.e., produced. The effect of capitalism is continuing economic progress, a steady increase in the quantity of capital goods available at a lower price. This naturally leads toward a continuous improvement in the general standard of living.

When profits are high competition flourishes. Free competition rewards the best and most efficient producers. Competition keeps prices low.

High profits attract more competition so a business can only corner a market temporarily. The corner or monopoly is thus broken and prices are again competitive. The consumer benefits the most. "Antitrust" is a term used by government to show distrust towards capitalist businesses. The consumers trusted these businesses allowing them to grow into "big" business. To break up one, highly efficient company into several, smaller, less efficient companies, which by necessity must charge higher prices, is absurd. Business is built on mutual trust. Consumers' trust in a product earns business profits. Profits attract new capital, new ideas and new businesses, competition flourishes, and monopolies are prevented; the one who benefits the most is the consumer. The consumer's money goes farther because prices are lower. (In a free market, monopolies, i.e. United States Postal System, can exist only as a special privilege granted by government.)

The consumer is captain of the economy. Profit and loss are the devices by which he exercises his supremacy on the market. Profit tells the entrepreneur the consumer approves of his action; loss that he disapproves. By his buying or abstention from buying, the consumer determines what should be produced, in what quantity and quality. The consumer determines which producer will succeed and which will fail. The consumer makes rich men poor and poor men rich. Either the consumer decides or the government. The producer must comply with the wishes of the consumer. The market is inescapable; it is the supreme law. The market stops losses by withdrawing the factors of production from the inefficient who charge higher prices, and transfers them to the efficient producer, whose prices are lower. The market checks losses and eliminates waste. In the form of lower prices, the consumer again benefits.

Another important function of the free market is the division of labor. In a free market all those who want to work can find work. The market wage rate tends toward a level at which all those eager to earn wages get jobs and all those eager to employ workers hire as many as they want. It tends toward full employment. On the labor market there are buyers for every supply of labor offered. Abundance of labor can only exist temporarily in any one segment of the labor market; it results in pushing labor to other segments and thereby increasing production in that segment of the economy.

Under capitalism there is no mass unemployment. Unemployment is a result of government interference in the economy either by minimum wage laws which fix the wage rates at a higher point than the free market's prevailing rate or by allowing unions to force up wage rates. Unemployment has become a chronic or permanent mass phenomenon since government enacted minimum wage laws, full employment laws, and gave unions the power to force up wage rates. These are characteristics of government interference in the free market, not an effect of capitalism.

The benefits from capitalism have been nothing less than remarkable. Its driving force, the profit-motive, forces the businessman to constantly provide the consumers with more, better and cheaper products. Directed by the most energetic, far-sighted individuals; it results in mass production for mass consumption.

The laissez-faire ideology laid the groundwork for the Industrial Revolution. It blasted apart the system of castes, guilds and monopolies that had restricted and prohibited competition. It demolished the social order in which a constantly increasing number of people were doomed to abject need and destitution. The Industrial Revolution opened an age of mass production for the needs of the masses. The wage earners were now working for themselves; they were no longer working for other people's well-being. They themselves were the main consumers of the products from the factories. People thronged to the factories as the only way to improve their standard of living. As low as the wages were, they were a means of a better life. The industrialists did not and could not force anyone to work in their factories. Women, who had no food to feed their children, and children, who were destitute and starving, fled to the factories. It was their only refuge. "It saved them, in the strict sense of the term, from death by starvation."[6]

Capitalism created the greatest environment of freedom known to man. It produced geniuses, men who pioneered in the arts and sciences. It raised the standard of living to unprecedented heights. It gave the world nearly one hundred years of peace. It has proven that man, when allowed to live by reason and to plan his own life, will create and produce in order to improve his standard of living.

Man, by choice, is moral. He lives for his own interest, not as a sacrificial animal for the benefit of government or society. Reasoning, creating man can only exist in a free society.

Understanding its true meaning, Americans should be proud to wear the title "Capitalists." It tells the world one comes from a country where men are free—free to think, to plan, to act, to keep the fruits of their labor—a country that upholds and protects individual rights. It tells the world that one lives under the only moral economic system—Capitalism.

6

WHAT IS SOCIALISM?

Socialism is not new. It grew and developed in the nineteenth century. By the turn of the twentieth century an immense majority of countries were already radical supporters. The Germans were firmly committed to the principles of Nazism—the German National *Socialist* Labor Party, where the common welfare ranked above the individual and private profit; "profit-seeking business harms the vital interest of the immense majority and that it is the sacred duty of popular government to prevent the emergence of profits by public control of production and distribution."[1] The Italians were more fanatical in their support of socialism. The Italian socialists named their party the Fascists. Fascism and Nazism were *socialist* dictatorships. Lenin had the grandest plan of all. He chose as the official name for his government—Union of the Soviet *Socialist* Republics. No reference to Russia or to the communists was made. He designed a name that would encompass the "socializing" of all countries. By the time the 1930s had arrived so had the American New Deal. Socialism had found its way across the Atlantic.

The characteristic marks of socialism are: dictators, wars, big governments, and inflation. Socialism is the opposite of capitalism. Socialism is a social system based on public ownership of the means of production. All material resources, including labor, are owned and operated by the government. The government is the sole employer, and no one is allowed to own more property or to better himself over and above what government allots him.

Because socialism is the enemy of capitalism and is being supported by Americans as the inevitable system of the future, Americans should have an opportunity to judge if they really want to switch allegiance from capitalism to socialism. This chapter studies socialism and the paragon of socialism—the U.S.S.R.

Not realizing their methods are socialistic, most governments, political parties, and labor unions are eager to restrict the sphere of private initiative and free enterprise. People are preoccupied with the social aspects of things, with government omnipotence and government measures. They expect everything from authoritarian action and very little from the initiative of enterprising citizens. They ignore or overlook the unprecedented and unparalleled achievements of the United States as a result of private enterprise. The United States was founded by individual citizens using their own initiative, intellect, wealth and courage long before government established itself as overseer.

Capitalism, i.e., the free market, is generally unpopular today, and all of society's problems are charged to it. Socialism, some say, is fairer. These advocates of socialism can be divided into two groups. One group wants to improve capitalism by government interference with the market. They are called interventionists. They want to dilute capitalism with government planning and regulations resulting in a mixed economy—halfway between capitalism and socialism. The other group wants to use interventionism, a mixed economy, as a stepping-stone to full socialism, i.e., socialized healthcare. Interventionism and socialism lead to the same destructive end.

Socialism is the establishment of a governmental bureaucracy-run economy. All economic enterprises are departments of the government. The whole nation forms one single labor army with compulsory service and assignment; the commander of this army is the chief of state. Under interventionism, the mixed economy, the means of production remain privately owned. Although it appears as capitalism, it is still socialism. Government fixes prices, wages, and interest rates. Government decrees at what wages laborers should work and for whom. The central board of production management is supreme. The economy is directed by czars. All citizens are merely civil servants to the state. It is still a market economy, however. The government seeks to influence the market by intervention of its coercive power, but it does not want to eliminate the market (the golden goose) altogether.

Nonetheless, all the methods of interventionism are doomed to failure. In their quest to help the country and its economy via minimum wage rates, bailout programs, government-created jobs, taxation, and credit expansion, they actually sabotage it. With the excuse that their controls and regulations are insufficient to solve all the problems, they demand more power to solve the very problems they created in the first place. In the end, the market economy is slowly replaced by bureaucracies, and interventionism turns into socialism: economic disasters, chaos, and mass unemployment.

Most interventionists are driven by an envious resentment against those whose incomes are larger than their own. They speak of profit without dealing with its corollary, loss. Americans, however, do not fear nor are they envious of profits and successful businessmen. In fact, they admire, respect, and seek after success. Americans distrust those who downgrade "capitalism," because capitalism stands for a desire to achieve wealth through independent individual action. If Americans were presented with a clear-cut choice between capitalism and socialism, socialism would lose. Socialism is an alien philosophy to Americans; if it continues to dominate the thinking in the United States, it will destroy America's immense wealth and free society, which current Fed credit practices are doing. Also, if President Obama's goal to renegotiate the Kyoto Protocol succeeds, it will negate our constitutional sovereignty.

Some interventionists are shocked when confronted with the realism that their policies foster dictatorial tendencies and lead to totalitarian socialism. They sincerely believe they can create a fairer distribution of income. They fail to realize the various measures they suggest are incapable of producing the results they desire, and only produce a state of affairs worse than already exists.

To illustrate, the following example is an analysis of a typical case of price control. It deals with the milk industry.

> If the government wants to make it possible for poor parents to give milk to their children, it must buy milk at the market price and sell it to those poor people with a loss at a cheaper rate; the loss may be covered from the means collected by taxation. But if the government simply fixes the price of milk at a lower rate than the market, the results obtained will be contrary to the aims of the government. The marginal producers will, in order to avoid losses, go out of the business of producing and selling milk. There will be less milk available for the consumers, not more. This outcome is contrary to the government's intentions. The government interfered because it considered milk as a vital necessity. It did not want to restrict its supply.
>
> Now the government has to face the alternative: either to refrain from any endeavors to control prices or to add to its first measure

a second one, i.e., to fix the prices of the factors of production necessary for the production of milk . . . Thus the government has to go further and further, fixing the prices of all the factors of production both human (labor) and material. . . .

But when this state of all-round control of business is achieved, the market economy has been replaced by a system of planned economy, by socialism. . . .[2]

If the government, faced with its first failure, does not remove the price control and return to a free economy, it must keep adding more and more regulations and restrictions. A mixed economy proceeds to a point in which all economic freedom of individuals disappears. In the end a mixed economy always leads to socialism.

The waste and suffering socialism produces are unnecessary. Free enterprise is much more efficient and fair. Besides, Americans know there is no such thing as a "free lunch." They want to work for a living. They thrive on competition. They want no government favors, handouts, or charity. They can and have survived on their own initiative for over two hundred years. Government favors and special privileges are relics of history, the age of kings and czars. Americans want to succeed by their own effort and ability. They have what it takes to make it on their own.

Consideration of socialism is repulsive to the American way of life. Americans must understand the truth about their government!

When socialists talk of raising farm prices, raising wage rates, and essentially lowering profits, ultimately implies the government must force these changes on the free market. Yet the authors of these projects insist they are planning for freedom. This program of self-contradictory interventionism leads to dictatorship in the name of freedom. The liberty its supporters advocate is liberty to do the things they themselves want done, not the liberty for people to choice for themselves.

There can be no freedom to live where one chooses when government decides where one works. There can be no freedom to choose the career one wants when government is the sole employer and assigns the job one must perform. There can be no freedom of thought or action when government has the power to silence opposition, permanently. Within a socialist society, there is no room for freedom.

The meanings of the words socialism and communism are synonymous. Russia was named the Union of Soviet *Socialist* (not Communist) Republics. She, too, failed in competing with freedom.

When Lenin was recruiting communists, he failed in America. He realized the workers lacked the impoverished social standards because they had already achieved well-being and were too busy making money. It is a communist trick to incite envy in those with lower incomes against those with higher incomes, but it is still prevalent today. Capitalism, by raising the incomes and wealth of everyone, creates peace and justice, not social unrest and injustice.

Communists have their own way of quelling social unrest and injustice. Their idea of central planning results in dictatorship. Dictatorships always advocate dictatorship by their own group. In advocating planning such people always seek after their own good, not that of others. They never admit a socialist or communist regime is true and genuine socialism or communism if it does not assign to them the most eminent position and highest income. The essential feature of genuine communism is that all affairs are precisely conducted according to the ruling group's will and all those who disagree are forced into submission, often through violence. Dictatorships and violent oppressions of all dissenters are today exclusively socialist institutions.

Setting aside the political repulsiveness of socialism, for a moment, here is an illustration of the economic impossibility of socialism. The following commentary is taken from an editorial prepared by Alexander Sachs, internationally known economic adviser and industrial consultant, which appeared in the November 6, 1972, issue of *Barron's*. It was entitled "Desperate State—Disaster in Soviet Agriculture is Largely Man-Made."

The big Russian wheat deal that was consummated in the summer of 1972 was necessary, according to prevailing opinions, because of that year's Soviet crop disaster, which chiefly sprang from 'adverse weather conditions. While this has been a traditional excuse for disappointing harvests, the truth of the matter, according to Mr. Sachs, was the Soviet *socialized* and *collectivized* economic system.

For instance, the Soviet fire-fighting apparatus was seriously inadequate. The Soviets proved unable to cope with vast forest fires, which subsequently led to the evacuation of whole villages and the total loss of their crops. In the Asian regions, at other critical junctures, freight cars fell short of need, tractors and harvest machinery proved inoperative for lack of spare parts; trucks arrived minus vital parts, which, presumably, were stolen en route to meet deficiencies elsewhere.

Grain imports were being jammed by bad organization, non-cooperation between railway men and port 'authorities, and a shortage of boxcars. Railroad management in the first half of October delivered only forty-one per cent of the freight cars needed to move the grain. The cars eventually used were unsuitable, spilling grain along the tracks. It took longer to process the documents than to load the grain. This illustrated both the shortage of technical facilities and bureaucratic incompetence.

Mr. Sachs concluded, we are not dealing with a crisis predominately caused by bad weather, but with a more fundamental malignancy that is inherent in the Soviet system and its pattern of farming. State and collective farming has produced an agriculture hopelessly mired in sociological prejudice and isolated from factory and laboratory. The truly desperate state of the Soviet farm economy relates back to the Five-Year Plan. It is the very existence of such a Plan, contended Mr. Sachs, principally designed for the command-type of industrial production and burgeoning arms industry that hobbles the progress of Russian agriculture. Rooted in their economic administration is a hereditary class of political careerists. It is the sons and daughters (and now the grandchildren) of revolutionary leaders from whom the staff of economic administrators and planners is recruited. Loyalty to the party is the major requisite for industrial and farm management. Thus there is a permanent bar to advancement by ability. The revolution of 1917 and the collectivization of agriculture effectively aborted farm modernization and industrialization of the USSR.

As the Soviet regime proves, only nations committed to the principle of private property have risen above poverty and produced science, art, and literature. There is no experience to show that any other social system could provide mankind with any of the achievements from a free civilization.

One major objection against socialism is the lack of free market prices. The market prices for the factors of production are established by bureaucratic edit. It is impossible to rely on calculation when planning future action or determining the result of past action. A socialist management of production has no way to avoid squandering the scarce factors of production both material and human (labor). Chaos and poverty for all is inevitable.

Second, socialism is a less efficient mode of production than capitalism because it lacks the profit incentive. In a socialist society the standard of living of the majority of the people will always be lower when compared with conditions prevailing under capitalism. If the Soviet regime were regarded as an experiment, the result has clearly demonstrated the superiority of capitalism and inferiority of socialism.

Many socialists argue the United States has achieved so much affluence because of her immense natural resources, not her capitalistic economic system. But the facts do not bear this out. Russia's soil is much better endowed by nature than that of any other nation. It offers the most advantageous conditions for the growing of all kinds of cereals, fruits, seeds and plants. Russia owns immense pastures and almost inexhaustible forests. It has the richest resources for the production of gold, silver, platinum, iron, copper, nickel, manganese and all other metals and of oil."[3] It is not what a country has, but how it uses what it has. But for the despotism of the Czars and the lamentable inefficiency of the socialist system, Russia could have long ago enjoyed the highest standard of living.

There is an eternal conflict between capitalism and socialism. In this conflict everybody must take a stand. Either one is for economic freedom or one is for totalitarian socialism. The middle-of-the-road position, namely interventionism, is only temporary. Freedom is freedom—one cannot be part free and part slave. There is no such thing as "excessive" economic freedom. Each individual must choose between the market economy and socialism. Government can preserve the market solely by respecting private property, or it can interfere in the market with laws and regulations. Society is run either by the consumers through means of supply and demand in the free market, or by the government through force and coercion.

Freedom and liberty always mean freedom from government interference. The irreconcilable conflict between rule of law versus rule of men (government force), has been man's history with man. It was a long and hard evolution. The rule of law, or limited government, as safeguarded by the Constitution and the Bill of Rights, is the characteristic mark of the paragon of capitalism—the United States of America.

Freedom of life, liberty, and property is a sham in a country where economic freedom is prohibited. There must first be respect for private property before there is respect for other individual rights, such as, due process of law, gun ownership, and the right to be secure against unreasonable search and seizure.

These rights are a sham if government is allowed to seize private property for the public domain, or without due process of law. No other individual has that right. Trotsky summarized the socialist economic system concisely: "In a country where the sole employer is the State, opposition means death by slow starvation. The old principle: who does not work shall not eat, has been replaced by a new one: who does not obey shall not eat."

The socialist experience in Russia proves beyond a doubt that socialism results in a very low standard of living for the majority of the people and unlimited dictatorial despotism. If it were not for massive aid from the United States government, a Russian revolution probably would have freed her people long ago.

Socialism has conquered three-quarters of the people in the world because it has rarely and ineffectively been opposed. Americans who believe the socialist propaganda that bombards the news media and educational institutions are slowly allowing the socialization of America. Capitalism only leads to socialism when government is allowed and encouraged to interfere in the economy. We are told that we have a right to health care; there is no such right. Hospitals used to be for profit, until local government took over. The national healthcare crisis is a result of government wage controls and tax incentives in W.W. II. It was exacerbated in 1965 when government promised health care for 12 million seniors, thereby competing in the market and raising health insurance costs. Government goes from creating one crisis after another, always expanding its reach. Now it wants to solve the "crisis" by nationalizing healthcare (www.npr. org, 9/20/09).

The coming of socialism is far from inevitable. As Thomas Jefferson once declared: "An elective despotism was not the government we fought for." He warned that the only defense against tyranny is an informed electorate. It takes intellectual and moral courage to seek the truth. It will take courage to reverse the trend toward socialism and pave the way back to freedom. Reason and ideas determine the course of man's future.

Open and unrestricted recognition and support of capitalism is the only way to stop the trend towards socialism and tyranny.

7

CAPITALISM VS. SOCIALISM

The antithesis of capitalism is socialism. All socialist societies are fundamentally the same. The basic value of a socialist society is death, as opposed to life in a capitalistic society. Socialism condemns the idea that man possesses inalienable rights to life, liberty, and pursuit of happiness. The basic premise of man's morality is changed from man is an end in himself, to the premise that man does not live for his own sake, but for the sake of others. Its political corollary is dictatorship. Its economic corollary is socialism.

Under socialism the state is considered omnipotent and omniscient; it is supreme. There are no individual rights; the rights to life, liberty, and happiness are denied. There are no property rights. And beyond the sphere of private property and the free market lies the sphere of force and coercion. Individual freedom is denied. The only right allowed, because it cannot be denied, is the right to commit suicide. Capitalism is the only moral economic system because it respects individual rights and guarantees individual freedom. Socialism is an immoral system because it denies individual rights and prohibits individual freedom. A man with no freedom is a slave to those who control his freedom. Philosophically, the choice between capitalism and socialism is really a choice between freedom and slavery.

Socialism promises that if men will give up their individual rights to the state, the state will see to it that all men will be equal. Man will be free from want; he will be secure. The state will take care of everyone.

Another word employed to mean equal is egalitarianism. Socialists use it to mean not equality before the law, which already exists in the United States, but to mean inequality for all and equality and prosperity for the chosen few. Only capitalism protects the freedom, the rewards and the incentives for every individual's achievement, each to the extent of his ability and ambition, thus raising the intellectual, moral, and economic state of the whole society.

This chapter will prove that socialism produces not prosperity, but poverty, not security but insecurity. It will show how socialists try to subvert and undermine capitalistic societies, always with the excuse of "taking care" of the people or for the "public good."

Socialism produces poverty, hunger, and misery, nothing else. All promises to the contrary are lies. An economy is too complex for any government to manage successfully. There are three main reasons: first, no individual or government is omnipotent and/or omniscient; second, the purpose of the socialist government is to create stability, when in reality no stability exists; nothing is perpetual but change; third, it is impossible to satisfy all the consumers' demands. In a constantly changing world, man makes hundreds of thousands of decisions in his lifetime—some simple, some complex; some right, some wrong. No group can choose the right answer for thousands of decisions for millions of people.

Competition is the only way to efficiently meet consumer demands. Competition forces the businessman to constantly check his premises against his competition to see whether his idea really works. If it does not, then he goes bankrupt. If he is clever, he will meet the competition's challenge. Under socialism there is no competition to regulate government, or test its plans by a competitor. The government grants itself an unjust monopoly. There are only a few ways errors in government planning are corrected: depression, revolution, or war.[1] Free enterprise is exceptionally more efficient. Socialism forces all men to suffer with lower standards: all men are economically equal, equally poor.

The exception is the government elitist, who makes a handsome living interfering in our lives. They are bureaucrats, car czars, or administrations, such as the FDA, which isn't protecting us from drug companies, but sacrificing us to their greed. The August 15, 2009 issue of the *Daily Mail* warned of the relationship between the swine flu vaccine and nerve damage (www.mercola.com, 9/1/09). A German scientist has linked swine flu vaccine to cancer cells (www.mercola.com, 9/8/09). We are being subjected to vaccine induced diseases, which they've done before (www.healthfreedomalliance.org, 8/26/09). Pfizer was fined $2.3 billion for illegal marketing practices of its drugs. The Czech Republic cancelled its flu vaccine order from Baxter Labs because Baxter wouldn't guarantee safety. States are enacting emergency health powers acts, training police, and readying rfid bracelets in anticipation of a flu epidemic in the name of Homeland Security, which is an assault on our civil liberties (www. healthfreedomalliance.org, 8/13/09, 9/18/09). But the majority of the people are unaware of these tyrannical dangerous government policies.

The foremost tool socialist governments use to gain control over an economy and the people is the banking system. The fifth plank of Karl Marx's Communist Manifesto reads: "Centralization of credit in the hands of the state, by means of a national bank with state capital and an exclusive monopoly." Lenin said the establishment of a central bank is ninety per cent of communizing a country. This is underscored by the observation of Reginald McKenna, President of the Midlands Bank of England: "Those that create and issue the money and credit direct the policies of government and hold in their hands the destiny of the people." Amachel Rothschild was quoted as saying: "Give me the power to issue a nation's money; then I do not care who makes the laws." The Founding Fathers were aware of the threat of a central bank. Thomas Jefferson wrote to John Adams: ". . . I sincerely believe, with you, that banking establishments are more dangerous than standing armies . . ." President Andrew Jackson on July 10, 1832, stated that the Bank of the United States, was "unauthorized by the Constitution, subversive of the rights of the States, and dangerous to the liberties of the people." Then he abolished the bank.

But as a result of a series of economic disasters[2], Congress passed the Federal Reserve Act of 1913. This act was to eliminate future economic disasters, no more boom and bust cycles, only steady growth and perpetual prosperity. The Federal Reserve Act nationalized the banking system of the United States.

The federal government essentially has three methods available to fund all its activities and programs. The government can confiscate wealth directly through taxes, it can issue debt, and it can print currency, i.e., inflation. Congress manages taxes, the Treasury manages the debt and the Federal Reserve manages our fiat currency.

Debt monetization is when the Treasury issues debt bonds, to the open markets and the Federal Reserve, with printed money, purchases these same bonds out of the open markets. The process is as follows: the Treasury sells a bond to company A in the open market. The government through the Treasury now owes company A the value of the bond plus interest. The Fed, with money it created out of thin air by printing, buys this bond from Company A. Company A was paid with printed money increasing the money supply leading to inflation. The Fed now owns the bond and is owed the value of the bond plus interest by the Treasury. The government now owes itself money and in the process has pumped more fiat money into the open markets. It is a shell game. Government moves debt from one hand to the other, paying for its expenses by increasing the money supply and inflation.

The Federal Reserve controls the nation's fiat currency and many aspects of our markets through its monetary policy set by the Federal Open Market Committee (FOMC). Traditionally the FOMC sets monetary policy which is executed by the Fed through manipulation of the federal funds rate. The Federal Funds rate is the interest rate private banks loan their excessive funds, stored at the Federal Reserve overnight to other private banks. Through manipulating this interest rate, the Fed is able to encourage or discourage banks from lending. Interest rates are a powerful indicator in capitalist markets by directing investment and entrepreneurs, but through the Fed's manipulation they become distorted and result in booms and bubbles followed by busts and recessions. This business cycle explanation is detailed by Austrian economists like Murray Rothbard. The Fed should not have a monopolistic power to control interest rates. It is a form of central planning, socialism, to artificially set interest rates. Interest rates should be determined by free open markets, not a select group of individuals like the FOMC.

To compound the danger of the Federal Reserve manipulating interest rates at its will, there is no transparency. Congress and the Treasury report to the people. The Federal Reserve's monetary policy, its management of the economy, and the Fed's ability to print currency, are all legally prohibited from being audited. The Fed is not required by law to reveal and rarely reveals loan negotiations, motivations or details. All the loans and emergency funding negotiations, in behalf of the taxpayer, happen in secrecy with no transparency to question its accuracy. When private individuals are not willing to risk their capital for a business, the government should not be allowed to risk the taxpayers' capital. The Fed can adjust interest rates and print currency for any reason it chooses and it is not accountable to anybody.

The unconventional monetary policy implemented by the Federal Reserve starting in 2008 has been unprecedented. The Federal Reserve's balance sheet has expanded from roughly $900 billion on August 7, 2008 to $2 trillion on September 3, 2009.[3] There have been many different funding activities during the financial crisis of 2008 engaged in by the US government, the Treasury, FDIC and the Federal Reserve. In many instances the Federal Reserve has served the role of an off government balance sheet lender. All the activities the Fed has engaged in, AIG asset purchases, Bank of America, Citigroup and Bear Stearns back stop loans, Term Asset-backed securities loan facility, commercial paper funding facility, etc, are allowed under the Federal Reserve Act Section 13 paragraph 3.

In 1932, the Emergency Relief and Construction Act, a highway construction bill, had tucked away and hidden section 13 paragraph 3, an amendment giving the Fed authority to lend to banks in emergencies. The FDIC Improvement Act in 1991 amended the same paragraph 3 allowing the Fed to lend directly to nonbank firms during emergencies, designating it the lender of last resort. As of September 2009, paragraph 3 grants legal authority for the Fed to provide funding for any business, bank or nonbank, which can not otherwise secure adequate funding from other banking institutions. By abrogating the functions of capitalism, the Fed has instituted socialism where government, or its representative, decides who succeeds and who fails. This is immoral and unconstitutional. The very least we should do is repeal paragraph 3.

By 1973 the Federal Reserve had created eight recessions and the worst inflation and depression the United States had experienced in modern times. Since Woodrow Wilson took his oath of office the gold supply has been mortgaged at least seven times over and the silver had all been sold. The treasury has been looted.

By the summer of 2009, the current recession is the worst in modern history. The national debt has risen to $11 trillion. Last year's federal deficit was $459 billion. The White House and the non-partisan Congressional Budget Office (CBO) project the federal deficit for fiscal year 2008-2009 to be $1.6 trillion, a record high or 11.2% of GDP. The CBO projects unemployment to reach 9.3% by the end of 2009 and to average 10.2% for 2010. The CBO projects the 10 year deficit to 2019 will be $7.14 trillion.

When the power of creating money and credit was recognized, the banking system was seized as a government monopoly. This is the strongest and most difficult monopoly to break up. The Fed is so powerful that Congressman Wright Patman, former Chairman of the House Banking Committee, who fought against the Fed for decades, said: "In the United States today we have in effect two governments...We have the duly constituted Government. Then we have an independent, uncontrolled and uncoordinated government in the Federal Reserve System, operating the money powers which are reserved to Congress by the Constitution." The Federal Reserve handles hundreds of billions of dollars of government and individual money, and its books have never been audited by government officials in its ninety-six years of existence. In 1964, Chairman Patman had been trying to persuade Fed officials into "permitting" a government audit. In 2009, Congressman Ron Paul is pushing for transparency in HR 1207. On March 10th, Rep. Paul in Congress said this about the Fed, "They get to create their money out of thin air, and spend it. They have no responsibility to tell us anything. Under the law, they are excluded from telling us where and what they do... they are supporting all their friends and taking care of certain banks and certain corporations. This, to me, has to be addressed." Americans have a right to know how their government is spending their money. The only way for Americans to know the truth is through an audit of the Fed. Hearings on HR 1207 began September 25, 2009.

The Federal Reserve did not delude all Congressmen. Congressman Charles A. Lindbergh, Sr., father of the famous aviator, told Congress: "This act establishes the most gigantic trust on earth. . . The new law will create inflation whenever the trusts want inflation." Henry Cabot Lodge, Sr., proclaimed: "The bill as it stands seems to me to open the way to a vast inflation of the currency. . . I do not like to think that any law can be passed which will make it possible to submerge the gold standard in a flood of irredeemable paper money." (*Congressional Record*, June 10, 1932.)

In 1933, President Roosevelt with one stroke of the pen, confiscated the gold holdings of all U.S. citizens, abolished the gold standard, devalued the dollar, and ushered in a new era of big government—the age of American socialism.

Once the banking system is under government control, manipulation of the money supply and credit begins through inflation. Inflation is caused by an increase in the supply of money and credit. As more money is printed, the value of each existing unit decreases. Inflation is currency debasement and depreciation. It is a government-created hidden tax on the hard working unsuspecting citizen.

Keynesian economists promise credit expansion will produce plenty of capital goods, lower interest rates, lavish government spending, full employment, redistribution of the wealth by expropriating the wealth of the capitalists, everlasting booms, and general prosperity. This is nonsense. When Keynesians promise to make everybody prosperous by increasing "credit," they are saying the way to prosperity is to increase debt. When they promise full employment by increasing wage rates, they are saying the way to full employment is to increase costs of production. When they promise to increase the national wealth by paying out government subsidies, they are saying that the way to national wealth is to increase taxes.[4]

Lord Keynes's economic philosophy has bankrupted the United States. As a socialist, Keynes promised something for nothing—a promise that many politicians could not pass up. Honest men do not lie and cheat.

Inflation is an underhanded conniving scheme. Politicians, says Henry Hazlitt, "talk of inflation as if it were some horrible visitation from without, over which they had no control—like a flood, a foreign invasion, or a plague. ... Yet the truth is that political leaders bring on inflation by their own monetary and fiscal policies."[5]

Here is how it works:

> Let us assume that the government issues an additional quantity of paper money. The government plans either to buy commodities and services or to repay debts incurred or to pay interest on such debts. However this may be, the treasury enters the market with an additional demand for goods and services; it is now in a position to buy more goods than it could buy before. The prices of the commodities it buys rise. If the government had expended in its purchases money collected by taxation, the taxpayers would have restricted their purchase and, while the prices of goods bought by the government would have risen, those of other goods would have dropped. But this fall in the prices of goods taxpayers used

to buy does not occur if the government increases the quantity of money at its disposal without reducing the quantity of money in the hands of the public. The prices of some commodities—viz., of those the government buys —rise immediately, while those of the other commodities remain unaltered for the time being. But the process goes on. Those selling the commodities asked for by the government are now themselves in a position to buy more than they used previously. The prices of the things these people are buying in larger quantities therefore rise too. Thus the boom spreads from one group of commodities and services to other groups until all prices and wage rates have risen. The rise in prices is thus not synchronous for the various commodities and services.[6]

The boom can last only as long as the credit expansion progresses at an ever accelerated pace. When the public finally wakes up, it realizes that inflation is a deliberate policy and prices will go up endlessly. The ultimate reaction of the public is the "flight into real values." They frantically exchange paper money for goods in an attempt to salvage some of their capital. Within a very short time, the paper money that was used as a medium of exchange is no longer acceptable. It has become worthless. This is the process of inflation which leads to the complete breakdown of the whole monetary system, including credit and banking. Inflation cannot be a permanent policy because it must result in a complete annihilation of the currency. This is where we stand today. Our banks and credit markets are in shambles due to the excesses of the Fed. This country cannot remain free if the Federal Reserve is permitted to exist.

The results of inflation are disastrous to the markets, the economy, and to the individual investor and saver. Inflationary policies result in a sense of false prosperity. Capital is wasted; all markets are impaired. Debtors profit and are favored at the expense of creditors. Excessive debt, leverage and extravagance are encouraged; savings and investments discouraged. Some individuals are enriched, some impoverished. Inflation makes it possible for some people to get rich by speculation and windfall instead of by hard work. People on fixed incomes are hurt the most. It rewards gambling and penalizes thrift. It promotes squandering, envy, resentment, corruption, crime, and in a blind effort to curb all these negative effects there occurs an increasing drift toward more government intervention, finally ending in dictatorship.

The public is morally ravaged. They are despondent and dispirited. The more optimistic they were under the illusory prosperity of the boom, the greater is their despair and their feeling of frustration, i.e., panic of 1929. Their trusted officials have robbed them of their earnings and savings. But the blame is placed on the people, speculators, or bankers instead of the real culprit—government. The final outcome of credit expansion is general impoverishment. The government, meanwhile, uses this immoral act of inflation for its own expansion to nationalize banks and car companies, pushing its agenda to nationalize healthcare, ever expanding its control, influence and empire.

Inflation is a lethal weapon in the hands of socialists. It enables government to bleed a country of prosperity, expand its power and demoralize its people. The German hyper-inflation of 1922-23 ruined its economy and demoralized the people, paving the way for Hitler. The hyper-inflation in China after World War II paved the way for Mao Tse-tung. And herein lays the insidious threat of inflation. History shows the chances of a country staying free after hyper-inflation are very small indeed.

Henry Hazlitt maintains that if the inflationary trend continues in this country, chronic deficits and a budget out of control will accelerate to the rate of inflation similar to the kind endemic in South America, leading to a collapse of the dollar.[7]

When the inflationary boom ceases, the currency has been destroyed, credit and business ruined. Depression sets in. This is the boom and bust cycle, produced not by capitalism, but by socialists central bank's inflationary policy.

A depression is a necessary although unpleasant process by which an economy recovers, throws off the excesses and distortions of the previous inflationary boom, and reestablishes a sound economic condition. The sooner the depression-readjustment is over with, the better. But socialists use this period to blame capitalism for the depression and through increased regulations add more controls to their stranglehold on the economy. By lending money to unsound business through bail-outs, propping up wage rates and housing prices, forcing interest rates down, or through increasing the money supply, government prolongs the agony and converts a sharp, quick depression into a lingering, chronic disease.

Ludwig von Mises asserts that sound economics recommends neither inflationary nor deflationary policy. It does not allow government to tamper with the market's choice of a medium of exchange. It establishes only the following truths:

1. By committing itself to an inflationary or deflationary policy a government does not promote the public welfare …or the interests of the whole nation. It merely favors one or several groups of the population at the expense of the other groups.
2. It is impossible to know in advance which group will be favored by a definite inflationary or deflationary measure and to what extent….
3. … a monetary expansion results in misinvestment of capital and overconsumption. It leaves the nation as a whole poorer, not richer….
4. Continued inflation must finally end in the crack-up boom, the complete breakdown of the currency system.
5. Deflationary policy is costly for the treasury and unpopular with the masses. But inflationary policy is a boon for the treasury and very popular with the ignorant. Practically, the danger of deflation is but slight and the danger of inflation tremendous.[8]

In addition to inflation and depression to undermine capitalism, socialists employ taxation. The second plank of Karl Marx's Communist Manifesto encourages, "a heavy progressive or graduated income tax." Taxes are collected by a branch of government, which uses fear, intimidation, and "Gestapo" measures to force people to part with their property. Taxation is another way socialist governments betray their citizens. The servant becomes the master. In fighting profits through taxation, government deliberately sabotages the free market, private property and individual liberty.

The effects of taxation are more easily discernible than those of inflation: taxes take from one group and give to another group—rob Peter to pay Paul. Taxation expropriates from the successful producers, who are thus penalized. The more a man produces, the larger his tax burden, removing his incentive to keep producing. Taxation limits competition because new businesses cannot acquire wealth to expand and become big business. Old established businesses are privileged by the tax system. Progressive taxation thwarts economic progress.

The complexities of the personal income tax reward the dishonest and those with government influence, but burden the honest without influence. Personal income tax implies the government has ownership and claim over the lives and labor of the people it is supposed to represent and protect.

Private property and confiscatory measures are incompatible. Since taxation prevents capital accumulation and savings, which are essential to capitalism, taxes destroy capitalism. As Chief Justice Marshall observed, the power to tax, is the power to destroy.

It is argued that taxes are necessary to support the services of government such as the postal service. The postal service runs at a deficit (at taxpayer's expense) every year. Since government has interfered with the oil and gas industry, there have been shortages and higher prices. Since 1973 the United States has been at the mercy of unfriendly foreign countries to supply us with oil. Government policies are the cause of oil shortages and exorbitant gasoline prices at the pump. The government has been meddling in public education for 40 years; students' test scores are lower than ever and employers complain that graduates are not as educated as their international counterparts. The industries that are not controlled by the government have managed to serve the public exceptionally well: clothing, food, construction, and electronics, etc. The domestic auto industry has been uncompetitive for years due to government interference. Now it is bankrupt and surviving on government hand-outs.

The pharmaceutical industry spent $1.5 billion lobbying Congress in the last decade and in so doing has manipulated the government's involvement with medicine and secondarily reinforced our dependence on drugs through government policies. Pharmaceutical lobby spending from 1998-2007 has risen sharply from $67.5 million to $189.1 million, which indicates their "investments" have been paying off.

Among their top "achievements" so far, according to lobbying disclosure reports filed with Congress and accessed by The Center for Public Integrity, were: Blocking the importation of inexpensive drugs from other countries; protecting pharmaceutical patents both within the United States and abroad; ensuring greater market access for pharmaceutical companies in international free trade agreements. With their latest "deal," the drug companies are continuing to ensure their lucrative business is protected, and any future health care reform does not cut into their profits.

Other socialist measures are government subsidies, tariffs, quotas, nationalization, and minimum wage laws. Subsidies, quotas, and tariffs benefit one group at the expense of another. For example, read about the tire tariff that President Obama just concluded in "President Obama Subsidized President Obama with Tire Tariff" by Daniel Ikenson, www.cato. org, 9/14/09. Government employs these means with the excuse they are protecting a vital industry. This is impossible, as illustrated by this basic lesson regarding capitalism:

When a capitalistic economy faces problems, it must face them with capitalistic measures—that is, increase the flow of capital spending (not government spending). Capitalistic problems cannot be cured with socialistic remedies... Experience indicates that even in socialistic societies, the device of government spending does not cure—it merely relieves the condition temporarily.[9]

Government cannot run a business at a loss or subsidize an unprofitable project unless it withdraws the means from taxpayers by taxation. When the government collects taxes and spends more, taxpayers have less to spend. When there is no profit-motive, responsibility is dissipated among bureaucratic rules and regulations. The results of centralization and nationalization policies are political corruption, poor service and financial failure. England once nationalized its banking system, but failing to make it work had to turn it back over to private enterprise.

Minimum wage laws are a good example of the subversive effect of government interference. In a free market all those who want to work and those who want to employ workers are able to meet their needs. When government decides that the lower wage earner's earnings are too low and passes legislation to increase his earnings, it raises the wage rate level above the free market wage rate level. Business must operate for a profit so jobs are reduced or higher prices are charged. The higher the minimum wage, the higher the unemployment. The consumer pays more for the same product. Thus, minimum wage laws cause chronic unemployment (in the unskilled labor force) and higher costs.

The Federal Reserve Act, prohibition of gold money, inflation, taxation, nationalization, and regulations are inherent ways socialists undermine capitalism and freedom. They all involve the same principle: government's disrespect for private property, the free market and individual rights.

These acts and programs have been tolerated and even encouraged because some people are under the misunderstanding that the function of government or the right of government is to expropriate the wealth of the privileged and distribute it among the underprivileged. They term this the "fair" redistribution of the national income. The answer is, first, an intrinsic feature of capitalism is that wealth is owned unevenly. Nikolai Lenin appreciated this fact when he observed that "uneven economic and political development is an absolute law of Capitalism." Second, it is nonsensical to try to figure the national income or national wealth. An individual can convert his property into money, but a nation cannot. Third, within a capitalistic economy goods are not first produced, appropriated, and then distributed. There is no such thing as the appropriation of ownerless goods. Goods are produced and come into existence as somebody's property. If one wants to redistribute them, one must first confiscate them. Based on the right to property, the redistribution of wealth by government is immoral. The government has nothing to give to anybody that it does not first take from somebody else. No government has the right to confiscate the property of one man in order to distribute it to another man. When one comprehends the full meaning of property rights, it is clear that most government programs, such as taxation, inflation, and subsidies, are violations of that right.

To sum up, socialism, by removing the rewards of thinking and action—the profit-motive and property rights—forces its citizens to become slaves to the state. The end result of socialism is progressing impoverishment; products becoming shabby because there is no reward or pride in workmanship; fewer products from which to choose because competition dries up. It is anti-survival, anti-life to work for the common good, to hold no selfish interest, to have no incentive to work. To the individual it means misery and degradation. Only the elite are enriched because, as parasites, they profit from the exploitation of the majority who work.

Socialism is sure death to a society. The last great Roman historian, Ammianius Marcellinius, blamed the decline in personal morality and self-determination as the causes of the fall of the Roman Empire.

> . . . the essential cause of Rome's decline lay with her people: their morals . . . their failure to do what was right, their desire to borrow on tomorrow and send the bill to others. . . Economic decay and political decay went hand in hand as they always have and always will. A decentralized social order was replaced by a centralized state-controlled economy and bureaucracy. . . The private citizen abdicated his responsibilities to a central government; and the cost of maintenance crumbled the Roman Nation.[10]

Under laissez-faire capitalism, personal morality and self-determination are an essential way of life. Business prospers. The peaceful coexistence of sovereign nations is possible. Under socialism it is impossible. Keynesian economics teaches that nationalism is the best internationalism, that hostile policies bring peace, and friendly policies, war, that international currency stability and free trade bring instability and chaos, and that nationalistic and mutually hostile policies bring international stability and prosperity."[11] This is irrational. Socialism fosters trade wars, foreign exchange controls, international hatred, and war. The philosophy of protectionism is a philosophy of war. Life and property are jeopardized. Socialism undermines individual integrity. In trying to make programs "fairer," Congress perpetuates injustices with more laws.

The principles of socialism are self-contradictory. No government can guarantee freedom and protect private property otherwise than by supporting and defending the free market. The substitution of big government and interventionist policies for the free market as practiced for the past seven decades by Western governments has resulted in wars, civil wars, ruthless oppression of free people by self-appointed dictators, economic depressions, poverty, mass unemployment, and disregard for the savings and pensions of the middle class.

The unsurpassed efficiency of capitalism has never before manifested itself in a more profound way than in this age of heinous anti-capitalism. While governments, political parties, and labor unions are sabotaging all business operations, the spirit of free enterprise still succeeds in increasing the quantity and improving the quality of products and in rendering them more easily accessible to the consumers. The majority of people in capitalistic countries enjoy a standard of living today far superior to ages gone by.

Nevertheless, capitalism is doomed if the actions which its functioning requires are rejected by a nation's morality, are declared illegal by the laws, and are prosecuted as criminal by the courts. The Roman Empire crumbled to dust because it lacked the spirit of free enterprise and embraced socialism. The policy of interventionism by ignorant politicians and presidents with executive orders are destroying our freedoms at an unprecedented pace.

There is a choice between the free market—capitalism, and bureaucratic whim—socialism. It is within man's power, says Henry Hazlitt, to avert the nightmarish prospect of galloping socialism, to restore order, justice, constitutionalism, limited government, economic and personal liberty, internal peace, and stable prosperity and growth.[12] Man cannot evade deciding between these alternatives by adopting a "middle-of-the road" position. Either Americans stand up for free enterprise or they succumb to more confiscation of their property. To abolish the free market means complete chaos and the disintegration of the division of labor as it is known today.

The American Revolutionary, Thomas Paine, once said, "These are the times that try men's souls." No doubt Ammianus Marcellinius had entertained that same thought. Today, men are contemplating the current state of affairs and think these are the times that try men's souls. All of them are correct. Man's struggle for freedom is eternal, which further emphasizes the importance of grasping how evil socialism is. Appeasement will not work; compromising will not work. Control is indivisible. Socialism means that one will alone chooses, decides, directs, acts, and gives orders. The substitution of economic planning for economic freedom removes all freedom and leaves to the individual only the choice to obey. There can be no compromise between capitalism and socialism. In any compromise between good and evil, evil always wins. Philosophically they are incompatible and irreconcilable. The difference between capitalism and socialism is the difference between freedom and slavery.

8

TO THE GLORY OF GOLD

The Founding Fathers were right about their suspicion of government. They tried to insure the usage of gold and silver money so future generations would not have to fear oppressive taxation and destructive inflation. But the Founding Fathers' great work—the Constitution—was subverted by government when the usage of hard money was prohibited, first gold in 1933 and silver in 1965.

When gold and silver are outlawed, when man is given no choice, when he is forced to accept paper money for his labor, he is robbed of his reward. The real money he should be receiving for his labor is reserved for governmental use, to be squandered as politicians decry. The individual is given paper money—which is inflated, depreciated, debauched, and debased. He is forced to accept paper as legal tender. He is forced because only by force will man part with his property.

The U.S. Treasury Department is in charge of interpreting the gold laws. According to the Treasury Department, Office of Domestic Gold and Silver Operations' statement of July, 1966, "The basic principles governing the administration of the Gold Acts and Orders are that gold, as a store of value, can be held only by the Government." In other words, the government has appropriated to itself the unconstitutional right to seize its citizens' gold—their wealth—and has left a counterfeit pile of paper. Due to the lack of transparency of the Fed and Treasury, individuals cannot realize how fast their paper money is being embezzled.

The only other major nation, besides the United States and Great Britain, which prohibited the ownership of gold by its citizens, was the Soviet Union. Private holdings or transactions in gold were considered by the Soviet Union to be "economic crimes"—most serious offenses in a communist-socialist state. Those engaged in them are subject to the firing squad.[1]

The importance of gold ownership is twofold. One, the only true economic barometer is gold. A free price system for commodities and currencies tends to keep the price of gold stable. Inflation forces up prices, including the price of gold. As gold appreciates, paper money depreciates. When the price of gold doubles in relation to the amount of currency, the value of the currency, or paper dollars, is cut in half. This devaluation of the dollar is the natural outcome when government inflates the money supply, thereby decreasing each unit's worth. Thus, gold can measure the extent of inflation.

One purpose of money is a store of wealth. By destroying gold's objective value, an equivalent of wealth produced, the government has the power to confiscate its citizens' wealth and property without their knowledge and consent. This is the second reason why gold ownership is important. Once people lose the intrinsic value of their money, they can expect to lose their freedom as well.

> Throughout history, fiat money and tyranny have gone hand in hand. For a recent example, that master of oppression, Adolf Hitler, waged a relentless war on gold to the very end of his brutal and despicable empire. Intrinsic-value money allows the individual to fashion, to a great extent, his own economic destiny; fiat money puts him at the mercy of the state; if the state is sole arbiter of value, then the state can change the value of its money or inflate the supply at will—and the citizen can go whistle for his lost savings. This rather obvious lesson of history was not lost on Hitler, who recognized immediately that gold was an enemy of the authoritarian state and consequently did his best to banish it from the Reich. Fiat money, in the final analysis, can circulate only by fiat, that is, by force, and it inevitably changes *any* republic into a despotism. People who allow their money to lose its intrinsic value, can expect eventually to lose their freedom as well.[2]

Another master of oppression was Benito Mussolini. He also understood the tremendous power that gold carries. Those who control it are in a position to dominate those who do not. As long as the control of gold is in the hands of the people, the people are safe; when the control of gold falls into the hands of government, the people lose their guarantee of safety. As soon as Mussolini became dictator, he confiscated all the gold and silver. To finance Fascist socialism and to build up his war machine, Mussolini ordered iron kettles to be placed in the streets of Italy. The people, walking by in single file, were forced to toss in the kettles their gold, silver, silverware, and jewelry.

A tyrannical government needs all the precious metals it can obtain to finance its wars. It must strip the people of their precious metals, their wealth. Should the people accumulate wealth, government either outlaws gold possession or floods the country with printing-press money, thereby reducing the value of the money and confiscating their wealth. For this reason, *gold* becomes the *natural enemy* of *socialism*. Sound money and big government cannot exist side by side. One or the other must go.

Private ownership of gold is essential to the maintenance of freedom. Why has the United States government been so adamant against the private ownership of gold? If gold were a "barbaric relic," as they claim it is, then why did they prohibit its ownership? It is unnecessary to prohibit the ownership of candles or the horse and buggy. After all, gold is a commodity just like any other commodity. What would happen if the government started prohibiting one commodity after another? If the government considers gold "demonetized," then why all the fuss about its ownership? In our enlightened age of civil rights, if people want to own gold, and who has more right to it than those who earn it, why not let them?

If the people were allowed to use gold as money, it would explode the lies they were told, and forced to pretend to believe, about paper money's real worth. When government makes crimes out of innocent and harmless actions, it must have an ulterior motive.

Since gold is money and money is the root of all good, then gold, too, must be the root of all good. An honest hardworking man should be allowed to own and trade gold as his right by virtue of being a free man and in order to remain free.

By what right does the government deny the private ownership of gold? If the government does not protect its citizens' rights, who will? And if it does not protect their rights, then who needs the government? The only valid justification of a government is the protection of individual rights. A right that is granted by the will of those who rule is no longer a right; it becomes a favor that is revocable at will. Since the Constitution specifically calls for gold and silver as legal tender, the government has overstepped its authority; it has no right to tamper with the market's choice of a medium of exchange, i.e., the private ownership of gold—an inalienable right.

Using gold as a medium of exchange allows free trade among free men, which is an essential part of capitalism. Capitalism develops respect for private property, a high moral fiber within the community, sound business practices, a high standard of living, independent men and women, and freedom and justice for all. Capitalism has created the greatest environment of freedom known to man. It gave the world nearly one hundred years of peace and raised the standard of living to unprecedented heights. Under the gold standard, the United States was known as the "land of opportunity."

Gold, more precisely the gold standard, was the medium of exchange by which capitalism brought science and industry into the remotest parts of the world, everywhere destroying age-old prejudices and superstitions, sowing the seeds of life freeing minds, and creating riches before unheard of. Gold and the gold standard go hand in hand with capitalism, which united all nations into a community of free nations peacefully cooperating one with another. The gold standard was the world standard of the age of capitalism. People throughout the world viewed the gold standard as the symbol of peace and prosperity.

The second half of the book will prove that whenever gold is traded freely, men remain free and economies prosper. Whenever a shortage of gold develops, usually as a result of individual hoarding due to a lack of confidence in government policy, trade slackens and economies stagnate. An acute shortage of gold can lead to a total collapse of civilization, such as the fall of the Roman Empire which precipitated the Dark Ages. The confidence that gold lends to trade is of crucial importance to all men.

In this eternal battle for individual and economic survival, in the name of justice and freedom for all Americans, there is only one weapon with which to fight the onslaught of socialism. This is the weapon that all socialists fear and is the first one they denounce. It is the last bastion of liberty and its final defense. That weapon is the Gold Standard!

PART II

THE GOLD STANDARD

9

THE ANCIENT WORLD GLITTERED WITH GOLD

For thousands of years, from the Orient to Egypt, the ancient world glittered with gold. Above the walls of man's first cities gold shone from temple spires and towers that were raised to the sun.

Gold was the first precious metal to attract the attention of man because it is one of the few metals found in the elemental or free state in nature. Gold nuggets were attractive because only gold exhibited luster and shone like the sun. It was almost indestructible and immediately useful.

When gold was discovered and man learned it was so easily shaped, shells, which were valued in ancient times, were reproduced in gold. This gave permanence, strength, and a new beauty to immemorially old forms of ornaments.

Metallurgically, gold offered minimal problems to early craftsmen. Although heavy, it is extremely soft. It can be cut with a piece of flint and pounded back together again. It can be pulled into wire to be used as pins and fishhooks. Its very permanence gave it a uniquely high position in the early scale of metallic values. As a substance it was very precious because it was very rare. It does not rust, corrode, or tarnish. Copper coins removed from hiding may show a heavy corrosive crust. Silver coins may show stains and tarnish until quite black. But gold coins will gleam as brightly as the day they left the mint, two hundred or two thousand years later.

Gold was regarded as more than a store of worth and as more than a measure of value.

> For it has been in a unique degree the decorative metal, loved by the great and wealthy as a means of ostentation, loved by the lesser man (according to his ability to acquire it) because of its beauty of color and sheen and texture in addition to its intrinsic value, and loved by the goldsmith because of its splendid working qualities.[1]

Since gold was almost indestructible, it symbolized life, and thus became the royal metal. Man searched for it, mined it, stole it, fought over it, and died for it.

Six thousand years ago the Egyptians used four-fifths of the world's gold to please their 2,000 gods. They used gold for religious purposes; it was divine. They displayed their wealth admirably by architecture, sculpture, and painting. This provides evidence of a continuing demand and a growing skill for gold.

The Egyptian rulers had a keen appetite for this precious metal. At one time Egypt had over one hundred gold mines in operation. It was the main source of gold used in antiquity. By royal privilege, the Egyptian rulers jealously guarded and monopolized the gold mines. Egypt's natural wealth was an important reason for the power of the successive rulers and of the continuity of the Egyptian culture.

As the Egyptian civilization advanced, her quest for gold increased. She intensified her search for gold with a resumption of foreign conquests. The royal metal became the reason for war and the prize of battle. To gain gold everything was risked and anything was fair.

From Egypt onward, civilizations began, grew, and perished according to their gold supply. Economies absorbed gold or were injected with it, gaining their wealth by increasing conquest or trade, or losing their wealth by sudden subjection. All the time the total quantity of gold in existence mounted steadily and massively.

Persia conquered Egypt. She took over the gold mines and hoarded the gold. She monopolized and immobilized the world's gold supply for the greater part of two centuries.

Alexander the Great conquered Persia. He seized the royal treasure of Susa and took over its contents: 2,000,000 pounds of gold and silver in the form of ingots and 500,000 pounds of gold coin. Such was the wealth of Persia, which, Greece, a poor nation subsisting on silver, conquered. Gold poured into the world's markets. The center of gold flowed from Asia to Europe, where it remained until the collapse of the Roman Empire.

Around that time pellets of gold and silver alloy were being used as the medium of exchange. But the intrinsic gold-silver proportion of this money could not be easily and accurately assessed. One of the kings of Lydia, Croesus, realized that commerce could be expanded and accelerated by the introduction of an internationally acceptable currency. He introduced a pure gold coin and a pure silver coin, both marked with his royal device of the facing heads of a lion and a bull. In 700 B.C., Croesus originated the world's first true coinage.

The coinage of gold, standardizing the currency, along with the conquests of Alexander the Great released great quantities of gold into the world's markets. As gold began to circulate, it stimulated trade through uniting many previously separated markets. Substitutes like silver became acceptable and were no longer discriminated against. Merchants were not forced to restrict their trading to where one metal was available or the other acceptable. They were free to roam the world. Thus, trade expanded and the merchant nations of the West prospered.

The expansion of the Roman Empire required vast supplies of gold. Rome's dependence on gold was reflected in that one gold-producing country after another was annexed until, at its peak, the empire included every source of gold then known to the Western world. Gold enabled Rome's trade to flourish. By buying off foreign mercenaries with gold, Rome protected her borders from foreign invasion.

Under Julius Caesar the denarius, a small silver coin, was originated. It was practically pure silver, equivalent to ten pieces of copper. By Nero's time the non-silver content in the denarius was ten per cent; under Commodus, thirty per cent, under Septimius, fifty per cent. By A.D. 260 the silver content of the denarius was only five percent. The decreasing amount of silver in the coin meant a profit to the Imperial mint, which was issuing unprecedented quantities of cheap coin.

The state compelled the acceptance of these debased coins at their face value through legal tender laws instead of at their actual worth. This practice in Egypt brought about inflation which ran out of control. A measure of wheat that had cost eight drachmas in the first century cost 120,000 drachmas at the end of the third century. The empire had begun with urbanization and civilization; it was ending in ruralization and barbarism.

Rome started as a Republic with independent, self-reliant citizens. In 27 B.C. she was turned into an Empire by Augustus, who managed to get all the power in his own hands by cheating the people of their freedom. Brian Bex, in his *The Decline and Fall of the American Republic*, likens it to the old "shell game": "The pea of real power was removed from the shell marked 'Republic,' to the one marked 'Empire' so fast and silently that it fooled the onlookers."[2] The historian Gibbon in *The Decline and Fall of the Roman Empire* explains the technique:

> Augustus was sensible that mankind is governed by names; nor was he deceived in his expectation that the Senate and people would submit to slavery, provided they were respectfully assured that they still enjoyed their ancient freedom.

By A.D. 300 the Empire had decayed to the extent where Diocletian substituted a managed economy for the free market. As dictator he centralized the state, always keeping the constitution preserved in the Senate. He gave food to the poor at no cost to the recipient. He imposed complete state control over industry. The state became a powerful employer, and in some cities, the largest employer. Trade associations and craft guilds received various privileges from the state. He imposed wage and price controls. To support this bureaucracy—the court, the dole, and public works programs--taxation rose to unprecedented peaks. By the fourth century, a flight from taxes became almost epidemic.

By this time the silver and gold mines were drying up. The gold and silver Rome did possess were exported to China, India, and Africa as payment for the high living of the Roman emperors.

Deeply in debt, the government increased the minting of debauched coinage. The propensity of certain kings and emperors to devalue their coinage by clipping, filing, reducing, or debasing was prolific. The mighty emperors of Imperial Rome were particularly notorious for this dishonesty. The simplest and oldest variety of monetary invention is debasement of coins or diminution of their weight or size for the sake of debt abatement. The Roman authorities assigned to the cheaper currency units the full legal tender power previously granted to the better units.

This created soaring inflation and taxation; hoarding became commonplace. The people culled out the better coins that came into their hands, hid them, and passed along the degraded or debased coins. The hoarders of gold or silver coins were actually acting in self-defense. It was one way to hedge against continuing inflation and depreciation of the money.

The principle was later explained by an English economist named Gresham. Gresham's Law states: bad money drives good money out of circulation (into hiding). This economic law goes into effect whenever governments debase the currency. The ultimate results of the Roman emperors' interference with the free market and the money supply were steady economic and social disintegration.

The decline of Rome and the decline of its money went hand in hand. Rioting, lawlessness, dishonesty, and corruption were aggravated by the spectacle of emperors and governments who were little more than liars and embezzlers.

> From the economic crisis of the third century, largely induced by a corrupt money, the Western Empire never recovered. By the fourth century money had fallen to the degraded position of *ponderata* when it was customary to assay and weigh each piece offered in payment. And by the seventh century, the weights themselves had been so frequently degraded that it was no longer possible to make a specific bargain for money. There was no law to define the weight of a pound or an ounce and no power to enforce the law if one existed. Under these circumstances money became extinct. Nor, we are reminded, was it the only institution that perished; all institutions perished. There was no government except the sword, there was no law, there were no certain weights and measures, exchanges were made in kind, or for slaves, or bags of corn, or lumps of metal, which men weighed or counted to one another holding the thing to be sold in one hand, the thing bought in the other.
>
> No more fittingly can we close this comment on the failure of the Romans to cope with money than by quoting the words of one Antonius Augustus, cited by Del Mar, "Money had more to do with the distemper of the Roman Empire than the Huns or the Vandals."[3]

Upon Rome's collapse the barbarians who invaded Europe continued gold coinage of good quality. Although this released much gold currency, which, until then had been hoarded away out of fear and lack of confidence, gold coin minting, which had continued between A.D. 500-700 in France and Spain and briefly in Britain, ceased. By 700 there was not enough gold available to guarantee an economy based on gold coins. The gold supply had finally reached a point of scarcity where a gold currency was impossible. Coins in France were debased from gold to silver. This acute lack of gold in Europe existed for five centuries, from 700-1200.

At the moment of the collapse of the Roman Empire in the West, gold had been used for over 4,000 years to balance economies and to measure and store wealth. It changed form, but never perished. With the decline of one power and the rise of another, gold was always on the move. The gold which first belonged to Egypt, then Persia, then Greece, and later Rome, now flowed to the Byzantine Empire in the east, which unshaken by the collapse of the Roman half of the world, had embarked on a period of commercial prosperity.

The monetary lesson of Rome was well learned by Constantine, the founder of the Byzantine Empire. He learned that confidence in a government's honesty and integrity is the strongest type of power it can possess. Under Greek influence he established *a* new monetary system based on the gold coin—the *bezant*.

The bezant was minted at a standard of 65 grains of fine gold for *800* years—undoubtedly the most outstanding achievement in the history of money. So determined were the empire's rulers to maintain the integrity of their money that they required all bankers and others through whose hands money passed to take an oath never to file, clip or debase coins in any manner. The penalty for any violation of this oath: the offender's hand was cut off.

The Byzantine Empire survived for over 1,200 years, until A.D. 1453. Its people prospered; its culture flourished. No enemy dared attack its capitol. The bezant was the standard of value throughout the world. One of the most interesting lessons learned from the Byzantine monetary experience is that despite the constant and free export of bezants to all parts of the medieval world, there was never any "shortage" of gold.

The stability of Byzantium attracted the entire world's gold. The immense wealth amassed is almost incomprehensible by today's standards: Emperor Anastasius at his death in A.D. 518 left a personal treasure of 320,000 pounds of gold. Theodora in A.D. 856 handed over 109,000 pounds of gold and Basil II in the tenth century possessed 200,000 pounds of gold. Add the wealth in private holdings of 2,000 to 3,000 pounds of gold plus great stocks of gold held as church treasure and it is clear how the total wealth of the Byzantine Empire caused a gold famine that spread over Western Europe after A.D. 700.

During the Dark Ages, from 500-1500, gold virtually disappeared from currency; it was restricted by monarchies for the adornment of kings. The Dark Ages was a period of monetary debauchery throughout medieval Europe. In the eleventh century Byzantine currency debasement started. The gold then flowed back to Europe through trade with the Arabs and the crusaders. The transition of Europe from acute poverty to relative prosperity was a long and difficult process. By 1400, however, economies were expanding again. Gold was in great demand. Gold coinage started between 1324 and 1325. By 1500, Europe was again stocked with good supplies of gold.

Gold gave new life to commerce. Gold and silver were the values placed on new lands. Portugal received gold from Africa and Japan. Spain discovered vast supplies of gold in Mexico and South America. In the 107 years from Columbus' landing, the total gold brought back to Spain was 750,000 pounds. Emperor Charles of Spain monopolized the gold supply of Europe. He knew the joint prosperity of Spain and Europe depended on the prompt arrival of the treasure fleets.

Banking centers in Lisbon, Seville, Antwerp, Vienna and Genoa acquired great wealth by financing the trade which they stimulated. By then, any European nation of consequence had to present a gold currency that was not only handsome but profuse. The gold coins of Europe continued to increase in size. Henry IV of Spain issued a gold piece weighing half a pound!

The multiplication of gold supplies in the fifteenth and sixteenth centuries led to a position where control of the price and movement of the metal began to slip from the grasp of kings into the hands of merchant bankers and goldsmiths in the larger centers of commerce.

The people entrusted the private goldsmiths with their gold rather than an agency of the Crown. By leaving gold with goldsmiths in markets wherever they traveled, merchants found that a receipt signed by a known and trusted goldsmith of the community was as readily negotiable as gold itself. The receipts became the first bank notes—payable to the bearer on demand. They were supplemented by bills of exchange which instructed the goldsmith to transfer a part of the depositor's gold to the man who presented the signed note. The paper was lighter to carry, safer from theft, and could always be exchanged for gold when desired.

The smiths soon discovered they had more than enough gold on hand to cover all the receipts presented for payment at any one time. They started loaning out some of the gold at interest. Thus, the goldsmiths became the world's first bankers and the first to establish a system of credit. In addition, they gained control of the gold bullion market, which has continued to this day.

Following the Dark Ages great volumes of gold and silver were discovered. Since production still lagged behind the influx of gold, prices rose. The Industrial Revolution in eighteenth century England began a process by which Europe severed its bondage from the lever, the pulley, and the screw, and productivity swiftly regained a relationship with the growth in gold supplies. England became one of the foremost gold markets of the world.

In the meantime, gold had recovered its position traditional in ancient civilizations, which had been dislodged by the disorder and corruption of medieval economies. It had again become the universally prized metal and universally desired as a measure of value and as a store of wealth.

10

THE CALIFORNIA GOLD RUSH

The vast gold supplies found in Mexico, South America, Japan and Africa wiped out the deep poverty of the Dark Ages and lifted Europe into the era of the Industrial Revolution. Those discoveries were merely a prelude to the next El Dorado—the California gold rush of 1849, which is one of the most fascinating episodes in the history of gold.

Innumerable finds of gold of immense richness had been made throughout the 6,000 year history of gold. But none could match the California boom of 1849. It held limitless attraction to men from every part of the world; its vast wealth catapulted the United States into a world leader; the industrial developments brought forth from the mines launched the American Industrial Revolution era. Romantic tales of the Old West are a favorite subject to Americans of all ages.

The California gold rush was an unparalleled phenomenon in man's history with the precious metal. For the first time in history the gold belonged exclusively to the man who discovered it. The United States of America was a free country and California was a free territory; and the gold in this big country was free for the finding. It was the property of the man who found it, to do with it as he pleased. There were no kings, emperors, landowners, or governments demanding a share. What government agents did exist at the time was limited and ineffective. It was every man for himself and by 1849 there were 100,000 of them. Considered as a whole, the mass migration to California was on a truly colossal scale. Men came from the four corners of the globe, spoke a dozen different languages, and represented every walk of life. Some came halfway around the world passed Cape Horn, arriving at San Francisco in vessels that were, by then, only fit to rot![1]

The ambition of the California forty-niner was the fuel that started and propelled the California gold rush. He was a rugged individual, whose highest value was life and he loved the thought of striking it rich. For that goal he was willing to endure incredible hardships. His life consisted of hard physical labor, insufficient shelter of brush or canvas, and a diet that was monotonous and inadequate. He suffered from scurvy, dysentery, and typhoid.[2]

Food shortages, insufficient shelter, and diseases were a common threat to the forty-niner's life. But the protection of life and property, which was under his direct control, was effectively protected. The forty-niners formed an informal kind of government where no government or court system had existed. As a gold strike was made, they gathered together and agreed on the laws for each new district. These laws regulated the size and number of claims each man could stake and the way they should be marked. They agreed on the actions to be considered crimes and the appropriate punishment.

On Sunday when most of the prospectors were in camp, they held town meetings. The majority ruled and the decision was final. Since there were no jails, crimes were punished immediately. The most immoral crime was theft. A man who was accused of stealing tools or provisions from another man's claim could be tried, convicted, and hanged within an hour. If it were a lesser crime, the culprit might be banished from the district; or he was branded, so his criminal record was known to all who later met him.

It was a harsh sort of justice, but it was swift. The laws that were established were enforced. Law and order prevailed. Life and property were protected. A gold-rush chronicler, Bayard Taylor, reported, "The capacity of the people for self-government was never so triumphantly illustrated."

Were the forty-niners really fair? Most emphatically, yes! The national code of mining regulations the government drew up in 1865 incorporated the forty-niners' principles and provisions pertaining to mining and mineral rights. The national code of mining regulations from 1865 still governs the mining industry today throughout the United States.

The California gold rush represented private enterprise and markets functioning at their best. Privately mined gold could be bought by the state if it wanted to buy it. It was the century of individual freedom and enterprise later known as the age of the individual.

Although the miners' equipment consisted mostly of picks, pans, and shovels, the yield between 1851 and 1855 ran at a rate of *175,000 pounds* of gold a year, with a peak around 200,000 in 1853. At that time gold was selling between $12 and $16 an ounce.

The forty-niner's reward was just and immediate—value for value. Since he was free to produce, to trade, and to profit, profit he did. At Carson Hill, a nugget was discovered weighing 195 pounds and was valued then at $74,000. (A replica of the Carson Hill nugget can be seen at Knott's Berry Farm, Buena Park, California.) North of Carson Hill at Angel's Camp, a prospector named Raspberry dug $7,000 worth of gold in three days, opening the mine that eventually made him a millionaire.

Between 1851 and 1855, California produced what had taken ancient Rome half a century to win from northwestern Spain. In the ten years after the discovery at Sutter's Mill, California produced $555 million in gold. And it is said that there is more gold still in California than has ever been taken out!

For a quarter of a century forty-niners blazed trails across the frontier, opening up the West. As towns that followed the gold discoveries grew, civilization developed. In 1850, California gained statehood.

The forty-niners produced the gold that financed industry and commerce. Many industrial techniques were invented and developed in the California mines, such as mass production, the 24-hour day, and the division of labor; they changed craftsmen's shops into factories. Machines were copied topside to speed the production and distribution of the world's goods. From the mine came the steam engine, the railway, the subway, the elevator, the escalator, artificial light and artificial air.[3] The knowledge obtained from the California gold rush led to gold discoveries in Australia in 1851, in the Comstock Lode in Nevada in 1859, in South Africa in 1866, and in Alaska in 1897.

The ambition and courage of the California forty-niner not only benefited the industrious miner, but was of immense benefit to the United States. Following the gold rush era, the United States was to become the most productive and wealthiest country in history. In recognition of the California forty-niners' achievements, the railroad track that first linked the East Coast with the West was joined, in 1869, at Promontory Point, Utah, with a golden spike.[4]

The California gold rush launched the gold exploitation era. Henceforth, gold was more diligently sought in all parts of the world, and immediately exploited when found.

The first gold discovery was in Australia. The loss of people as a result of the magnitude of the emigration to California from Australia was worrying Australian officials. In 1851 Australia formed the Gold Discovery Committee. The Committee offered a reward of 200 pounds to anyone who discovered gold within 200 miles of Melbourne. Within one year it was claimed. Within the next ten years 1,750,000 pounds of gold were produced in Victoria. The discovery of one nugget in 1869 was appropriately named the Welcome Stranger. It weighed nearly 160 pounds.

In 1859, the Comstock Lode in Nevada only four miles long and lasting twenty years was the second discovery. It produced America's primary source of gold. Gold was also discovered in Colorado, Montana, and South Dakota, where old Homestake mine remained the only sizable producer of gold in the United States until it closed and was merged with Barrick Gold Corp. in 2002. Homestake's 8,000 foot deep mine is now used for science and engineering research.

In 1866, gold was discovered in South Africa in the world-famous Main Reef Group. In 1973 it took an investment of $50 to $100 million to dig the first ounce of gold from a South African mine, hardly the kind of cash a prospector carried around in his poke. The gold belonged not to a poor man with a pick, but to the investor with capital. The South African mines produced over a billion dollars worth of gold a year, almost eighty per cent of the output in the non-communist world.

The day of the poor man's mining was not quite over. One richer goldfield remained to be discovered where every man was free to dig for himself, to get rich, or in this case, to freeze. The fourth El Dorado was in Alaska. In 1897, Dawson City sprung up in the Klondike area of the Yukon River in Alaska, as near to the North Pole as northern Siberia.

Here cold was the enemy. A prospector's thermometer was unable to tell him how cold it was because at forty-two degrees below zero the mercury froze; kerosene refused to pour at fifty-five degrees; at seventy-two degrees below the pain-killer turned solid. If the Hudson's Bay rum froze, it was eighty degrees below and no one ventured outside.

Despite the cold, scurvy, and gangrenous limbs, the search for gold continued. Those who survived the winter to bring back their prize, stepped off the ships with missing and mutilated toes, fingers, ears, and noses, caused by the bitter cold of the north. But they carried gold.

Within two years, Dawson City produced $32 million worth of gold.

From 1850 to 1900, the estimated gold produced from these five major goldfields was 23,000,000 pounds or *twenty per cent of all the gold ever produced in the world to date.*

11

THE DOMESTIC GOLD STANDARD

Although gold was available during the American Revolution, the Continental Congress used fiat money as an expediency.

In the aftermath, the Founding Fathers supported the gold standard. Not passively or theoretically; they supported it in knockdown, drag-out fights in the political arena, including one rebellion. Jefferson and Madison, in particular, were hard-money men and campaigned vigorously for gold and against paper money.

They learned their lesson the hard way and learned it well. The four words "not worth a Continental" recall the runaway inflation that very nearly destroyed the American Revolution.

"Continentals" were the paper money issued by the second Continental Congress to finance the Revolutionary War. It began in June, 1775, when the Continental Congress voted the first and supposedly last issue of $2,000,000 of paper "bills of credit," to be redeemed in silver after 1779. It ended in 1781 when the issuance of state and Continental paper totaled $240,000,000 and $210,000,000 respectively. As with every path to inflation, the notes were at first issued in moderate amounts and small denominations. But as depreciation set in, larger and larger issues were made, at shorter and shorter intervals.

During those terrifying years, commodity prices soared. In 1777, a Bostonian wrote, "We are all starving here, since this plague addition to the regulating bill. People will not bring in provision, and we cannot procure the necessities of life." In the following winter, the army at Valley Forge suffered agonies for want of food, clothing and blankets that simply could not be purchased in the controlled market. At the same time Americans were selling food and goods to the British in nearby Philadelphia for hard money. By 1778, prices were up 480 per cent from prewar levels.

Inflation was out of control. As each paper issue added to the glut of dollars in private hands, Congress had to make the next issue substantially larger to pay for the same amount of supplies. The states were forced to make Continentals legal tender. Sellers were forced to accept the notes at face value or forfeit their goods in penalty. Price controls and ceilings had to be adopted, enforceable by stiff fines and imprisonment. These laws did more to keep goods off the market than to keep notes circulating.

Congress went so far as to declare ". . . that any person who shall hereafter be so lost to all virtue and regard for his country as to refuse to receive said bills in payment, or obstruct and discourage the currency or circulation thereof . . . shall be deemed . . . an enemy of his country."

It was all of no use. The people would not accept worthless paper in exchange for their valuable goods, even on penalty of death. By 1781, it took one thousand Continentals to buy one dollar in specie (hard money).

The Continental inflation caused immense losses and unquestionably prolonged the war by several years. It had so badly damaged the nation's ability to carry on the war that only loans from France in the latter years saved the Revolution. Robert Morris, a financial genius, was able to use the loans, mostly in the form of supplies, but some gold, to put the war effort on a hard-money basis, and thus helped gain the victory so long delayed by financial distress. Only when the inflation had run its full inevitable course did gold and silver coin "come out of hiding," as it always does after an inflation, to start the exhausted nation toward recovery.

The havoc of paper money during the war ruined the country's economy. After the war the economy suffered from deflation. The general complaint about private and public finance was that hard money was scarce and growing scarcer, and paper money, resorted to again in the 1780s in seven states, was a threat and growing more threatening. The critical problem was the alarming shortage of gold and silver money, or specie. The drain of specie kept the back country in a state of political and social tension. The balance of trade was so drastically against the United States that even the most solid merchants wondered how long Americans' credit would hold up in Europe.

To put an end to paper money, the Articles of Confederation, the first constitution of the original thirteen states, in 1781, prohibited the issuance of bills of credit by the national government. When the second and final constitution was adopted in 1787, the hard-money issue was still very alive. For "what John Jay derided as 'the doctrine of the political transubstantiation of paper into gold and silver' had a powerful appeal to men with crushing debts and unpopular taxes to pay and with no coin in which to pay them."[1]

James Madison came to the aid of the hard-money people. He defended the value of gold and silver money over paper money. On January 25, 1788, he wrote the forty-fourth letter of the Federalist Papers in which he eloquently and effectively summed up the justice only hard money can produce:

> The extension of the prohibition to bills of credit must give pleasure to every citizen in proportion to his love of justice and his knowledge of the true springs of public prosperity. The loss which America has sustained since the peace, from the pestilent effects of paper money on the necessary confidence between man and man, on the necessary confidence in the public councils, on the industry and morals of the people, and on the character of republican government, constitutes an enormous debt against the States chargeable with this unadvised measure, which must long remain unsatisfied; or rather an accumulation of guilt, which can be expiated no otherwise than by a voluntary sacrifice on the altar of justice, of the power which has been the instrument of it . . . the States . . . ought not to be at liberty to substitute a paper medium in the place of coin. . . The power to make anything but gold and silver a tender in payment of debts, is withdrawn from the States on the same principle with that of issuing a paper currency.[2]

The hard-money people were victorious. As a result of their persistent effort, Article I, Section 10, of the United States Constitution says: "No state shall . . . make anything but gold and silver coin a tender in payment of debts."

The honesty and integrity of men like Thomas Jefferson, who advocated a one hundred per cent gold standard, produced justice and freedom in the marketplace. Gold protected the working man from inflation; it enabled him to receive his wages or profits in currency of full value; it enabled him to save without having the value of his savings depreciate. Jefferson knew fiat paper money oppresses the poor and those on fixed incomes. It was paper that robbed the poor to give to the rich. Paper created an unearned transfer of wealth from the working and middle classes to the debtor and those who create the paper money—central banks and governments. Through paper money, the rich grow richer and the poor grow poorer. Only the gold standard insures economic justice by making these unearned transfers of wealth impossible. It protects the rights of the working and middle classes—the backbone of the nation.

Although hard-money was victorious over paper money, there was one more battle that remained to be won—defeat of the United States central bank. Jefferson welded the pro-gold interests into a powerful political movement against the paper money forces as represented by Hamilton and the proponents of the Bank of the United States. This battle raged for a generation and culminated in 1832 when Andrew Jackson vetoed the central bank's re-charter. He deemed it dangerous to the future of the republic.

With gold and silver as lawful money and the central bank of the United States abolished, the United States was on the gold standard.

12

THE INTERNATIONAL GOLD STANDARD

The magnitude of gold discoveries in the late eighteen hundreds made available to the world vast supplies of gold. This enabled most nations to adopt gold as their medium of exchange. By 1900, nearly all developed nations respected gold as money and trusted the gold standard as the only objective and effective method to secure their prosperity and the worth of their national currencies.

At the turn of the century practically every economist of integrity supported the gold standard. The reason was simple: when a nation inflated its money supply, prices rose, gold flowed out of the country, the country's gold supply was reduced, prices came down, and as inflation came under control, gold flowed back into the country, prices leveled off. Only the gold standard could protect the individual's wealth and the nation's prosperity from inflation.

The gold standard requires neither rules nor regulations, nor legislation or government control, merely the individual freedom to own gold. This freedom of gold ownership embodies the freedom not only to buy and sell for use in industrial production, but also to employ it in exchange as money. The gold standard is a monetary system in which *gold is proper money* and all paper money is merely a substitute redeemable in gold. Any paper money issued must be backed one hundred per cent by gold bullion or gold coins and be fully redeemable on demand into gold. Under the gold standard the United States dollar represents a piece of gold of a certain weight and fineness. The legal tender is gold. Money is gold and gold is money. Monetary freedom means the gold standard.

Monetary freedom in the United States was short-lived, however. The early history of the American currency clearly illustrates the danger of government interference in the free market's choice of a medium of exchange. Instead of leaving to the free market the function of determining the gold value of money, it was considered proper for government to interfere and regulate the money supply. Since governments were generally biased in favor of the largest possible money supply, which was thought to generate national wealth and prosperity, they favored a double standard in which gold and silver were legal money. Instead of letting both metals circulate side by side at ratios that were freely determined in the money market according to supply and demand, governments stepped in to regulate their mutual exchange ratios. This regulation was, of course, price fixing the metals in terms of each other. The inevitable failure of the regulated bimetallic standard due to the operation of Gresham's Law led to either the gold standard or the silver standard; and the fixed ratio between the two determined the outcome.

The first coinage ratio of gold and silver that Alexander Hamilton, Secretary of the Treasury, chose was fixed at 15 to 1. This ratio overvalued silver and thus drove gold coins out of circulation. When Congress became aware of the disequilibrium in the specie currency, it endeavored to legislate the country back to the bimetallic basis. Congress passed an act on June 23, 1834 which reduced the gold content of the dollar from 24.75 grains pure gold to 23.2 grains, but left the bullion content of the silver dollar unchanged. The reduction of the bullion content of the gold dollar changed the coinage ratio from 15 to 1 to approximately 16 to 1. Just as the earlier ratio had overvalued silver, the new ratio overvalued gold. Consequently, in time, gold began to replace silver as the standard money. Silver coins and silver bullion disappeared from circulation in the same way they have disappeared from circulation today. Except today overvalued copper-nickel coins have driven silver into hiding.

The Constitution had created a bimetallic system by making gold and silver tender in payment of debts. Instead of leaving well enough alone, the government, through legislation, interfered with the gold/silver ratio and forced first gold then silver out of circulation. This forced the banks to substitute gold reserves for silver specie and a single standard emerged— the gold standard.

The gold standard was honored until 1862, when Congress suspended specie payments to pay for the Civil War. In place of hard money, Congress enacted a legal tender law, forcing people to accept paper money, and the country entered the greenback era.

Although greenbacks were the only legal money in the Union during and after the Civil War, there was monetary freedom in California and Californians preferred gold. They continued to use gold as their money. Business transactions were conducted in gold and money substitutes, such as bank notes and deposits, payable in gold. Since the people were free to choose between paper money and gold currency, they naturally chose gold. This choice forced all issuers of paper money to make payments in gold lest their paper fall in utter disrepute and cease to function as money.

The Species Resumption Act of January 14, 1875, resumed specie payments as of January 1, 1879. It took four years to coin enough gold to return to hard-money convertibility. Knowing the government was minting gold at a prodigious rate to meet all demands, the people again trusted the government's integrity and ability to meet its published commitments. The confidence of the people had been restored by the government's actions to fulfill its earlier promise of redemption. There was no further crisis, no bank "run" and, as a result, the premium on gold disappeared at once. The gold standard was not officially resumed until Congress passed the Gold Standard Act on March 14, 1900, when the dollar became the "standard unit of value," of twenty-five and four-fifths grains of ninety per cent fine gold.

Several European nations had already adopted the gold standard. Great Britain, the leader in world trade and finance, adopted the gold standard nearly fifty years earlier. Great Britain ended up on the gold standard in much the same way as did the United States. By interfering in the money markets the British government unintentionally changed the "pound sterling" into the "pound gold."

France in 1867 made it clear only gold could provide the basis for a workable system of interlocking national currencies. Germany went over to gold after the Franco-Prussian War, Austria-Hungary after 1892, and Russia after 1897. They achieved a transition from other standards, silver or irredeemable fiat, through substitution. Silver or paper money was exchanged for gold through the operations of their central banks.

It was not monetary freedom that gave birth to the nineteenth-century gold standards. There was no laissez-faire in monetary matters during this century of individual freedom and enterprise.

> The demonetization of silver and the establishment of gold monometallism was the outcome of deliberate government interference with monetary matters . . . it must not be forgotten that it was not the intention of the governments to establish the

gold standard. What the governments aimed at was the double standard. They wanted to substitute a rigid, government-decreed exchange ratio between gold and silver for the fluctuating market ratios between the independently coexistent gold and silver coins. The monetary doctrines underlying these endeavors misconstrued the market phenomena in that complete way in which only bureaucrats can misconstrue them. The attempts to create a double standard of both metals, gold and silver, failed lamentably. It was this failure which generated the gold standard. The emergence of the gold standard was the manifestation of a crushing defeat of the governments and their cherished doctrines.[1]

By 1900, most of the leading countries of the world were on the gold standard. The international gold standard had evolved without intergovernmental treaties and institutions. No one had to make the gold standard work as an international system. The world had an international currency: gold.

The gold standard united the world as international payments ceased to be a problem. It facilitated world trade and finance, and promoted a worldwide division of labor. The gold standard encouraged exportation of capital from the developed countries *to* the developing countries, and improved the living conditions of millions of people.[2] People viewed the gold standard as the symbol of capitalism—of peace and prosperity.

It is easy to understand why every economist, at the turn of the century, supported the gold standard. For nearly one hundred years there existed the longest peace and the greatest prosperity in modern history as a direct result of the capitalistic system, whose medium of exchange was the gold standard.

13

ECONOMIC FREEDOM AND GOLD

The gold standard presupposes individual freedom, private property, and free markets. It provides freedom to all. It allows every man to be the master of his future.

Socialists seem to understand, perhaps more clearly than many defenders of capitalism, that economic freedom and gold are inseparable and each implies and requires the other. Socialists and big government unite in an almost hysterical antagonism toward the gold standard.

The gold standard is an integral part of capitalism and economic freedom. Understanding the specific role of gold as a store of value in a free society helps to illustrate this.

Alan Greenspan, who was President of Townsend-Greenspan & Co., Inc., economic consultants, before becoming Chairman of the Federal Reserve in 1987, wrote an excellent article, entitled "Gold and Economic Freedom." The following paragraphs are excerpts from his article, which explains the crucial role of gold in a free society.

> The existence of such a commodity [e.g., gold], is a precondition of a division of labor economy. If men did not have some commodity of objective value which was generally acceptable as money, they would have to resort to primitive barter or be forced to live on self-sufficient farms and forgo the inestimable advantages of specialization. If men had no means to store value, i.e., to save, neither long-range planning nor exchange would be possible. . . .

> [However,] if all goods and services were to be paid for in gold, large payments would be difficult to execute, and this would tend to limit the extent of a society's division of labor and specialization. Thus a logical extension of the creation of a medium of exchange is the development of a banking system and credit instruments (bank notes and deposits) which act as a substitute for, but are convertible into, gold.

A free banking system based on gold is able to extend credit and thus to create bank notes (currency) and deposits, according to the production requirements of the economy. Individual owners of gold are induced, by payments of interest, to deposit their gold in a bank (against which they can draw checks). But since it is rarely the case that all depositors want to withdraw all their gold at the same time, the banker need keep only a fraction of his total deposits in gold as reserves. This enables the banker to loan out more than the amount of his gold deposits (which means that he holds claims to gold rather than gold as security for his deposits). But the amount of loans which he can afford to make is not arbitrary: he has to gauge it in relation to his reserves and to the status of his investments.

When banks loan money to finance productive and profitable endeavors, the loans are paid off rapidly and bank credit continues to be generally available. But when the business ventures financed by bank credit are less profitable and slow to pay off, bankers soon find that their loans outstanding are excessive relative to their gold reserves, and they begin to curtail new lending, usually by charging higher interest rates. This tends to restrict the financing of new ventures and requires the existing borrowers to improve their profitability before they can obtain credit for further expansion. Thus, under the gold standard, a free banking system stands as the protector of an economy's stability and balanced growth.

When gold is accepted as the medium of exchange by most or all nations, an unhampered free international gold standard serves to foster a world-wide division of labor and the broadest international trade. Even though the units of exchange (the dollar, the pound, the franc, etc.) differ from country to country, when all are defined in terms of gold the economies of the different countries act as one—so long as there are no restraints on trade or on the movement of capital. Credit, interest rates, and prices tend to follow similar patterns in all countries. For example, if banks in one country extend credit too liberally, interest rates in that country will tend to fall, inducing depositors to shift their gold to higher-interest paying banks in other countries. This will immediately cause a shortage of bank reserves in the "easy money" country, inducing tighter credit standards and a return to competitively higher interest rates again.

A fully free banking system and fully consistent gold standard have not as yet been achieved. But prior to World War I, the banking system in the United States (and in most of the world) was based on gold, and even though governments intervened occasionally, banking was more free than controlled. Periodically, as a result of overly rapid credit expansion, banks became loaned up to the limit of their gold reserves, interest rates rose sharply, new credit was cut off, and the economy went into a sharp, but short-lived recession. (Compared with the depressions of 1920 and 1932, the pre-World War I business declines were mild indeed.) It was limited gold reserves that stopped the unbalanced expansions of business activity, before they could develop into the post-World War I type of disaster. The readjustment periods were short and the economies quickly re-established a sound basis to resume expansion.

But the process of cure was misdiagnosed as the disease: if shortage of bank reserves was causing a business decline—argued economic interventionists—why not find a way of supplying increased reserves to the banks so they never need be short! If banks can continue to loan money indefinitely—it was claimed—there need never be any slumps in business. And so the Federal Reserve System was organized in 1913. It consisted of twelve regional Federal Reserve banks nominally owned by private bankers, but in fact government sponsored, controlled, and supported. Credit extended by these banks is in practice (though not legally) backed by the taxing power of the federal government. Technically, we remained on the gold standard; individuals were still free to own gold, and gold continued to be used as bank reserves. But now, in addition to gold, credit extended by the Federal Reserve banks ("paper" reserves) could serve as legal tender to pay depositors.

When business in the United States underwent a mild contraction in 1927, the Federal Reserve created more paper reserves in the hope of forestalling any possible bank reserve shortage. More disastrous, however, was the Federal Reserve's attempt to assist Great Britain who had been losing gold to us because the Bank of England refused to allow interest rates to rise when market forces dictated (it was politically unpalatable). The reasoning of the authorities involved was as follows: if the Federal Reserve pumped excessive paper reserves into American banks, interest rates in the United States would fall to a level comparable with those in Great Britain; this would act to stop Britain's gold loss and avoid the political embarrassment of having to raise interest rates.

The "Fed" succeeded: it stopped the gold loss, but it nearly destroyed the economies of the world, in the process. The excess credit which the Fed pump into the economy spilled over into the stock market—triggering a fantastic speculative boom. Belatedly, Federal Reserve officials attempted to sop up the excess reserves and finally succeeded in braking the boom. But it was too late: by 1929 the speculative imbalances had become so overwhelming that the attempt precipitated a sharp retrenching and a consequent demoralizing of business confidence. As a result, the American economy collapsed. Great Britain fared even worse, and rather than absorb the full consequences of her previous folly, she abandoned the gold standard completely in 1931, tearing asunder what remained of the fabric of confidence and inducing a world-wide series of bank failures. The world economies plunged into the Great Depression of the 1930's.

With a logic reminiscent of a generation earlier, statists argued that the gold standard was largely to blame for the credit debacle which led to the Great Depression. If the gold standard had not existed, they argued, Britain's abandonment of gold payments in 1931 would not have caused the failure of banks all over the world. (The irony was that since 1913, we had been, not on a gold standard, but on what may be termed "a *mixed* gold standard"; yet it is gold that took the blame.)

But the opposition to the gold standard in any form—from a growing number of welfare-state advocates—was prompted by a much subtler insight: the realization that the gold standard is incompatible with chronic deficit spending (the hallmark of the welfare state). Stripped of its academic jargon, the welfare state is nothing more than a mechanism by which governments confiscate the wealth of the productive members of a society to support a wide variety of welfare schemes. A substantial part of the confiscation is affected by taxation. But the welfare statists were quick to recognize that if they wished to retain political power, the mount of taxation had to be limited and they had to resort to programs of massive deficit spending, i.e., they had to borrow money, by issuing government bonds, to finance welfare expenditures on a large scale.

Under a gold standard, the amount of credit that an economy can support is determined by the economy's tangible assets, since every credit instrument is ultimately a claim on some tangible asset. But government bonds are not backed by tangible wealth, only by the government's promise to pay out of future tax revenues, and cannot easily be absorbed by the financial markets. A large volume of new government bonds can be sold to the public only at progressively higher interest rates. Thus, government deficit spending under a gold standard is severely limited.

The abandonment of the gold standard made it possible for the welfare statists *to use the banking system* as a means to an unlimited expansion of credit. They have created paper reserves in the form of government bonds which—through a complex series of steps—the banks accept in place of tangible assets and treat as if they were an actual deposit, i.e., as the equivalent of what was formerly a deposit of gold. The holder of a government bond or of a bank deposit created by paper reserves believes that he has a valid claim on a real asset. But the fact is that there are now more claims outstanding than real assets.

The law of supply and demand is not to be conned. As the supply of money (of claims) increases relative to the supply of tangible assets in the economy, prices must eventually rise. Thus the earnings saved by the productive members of the society lose value in terms of goods. When the economy's books are finally balanced, one finds that this loss in value represents the goods purchased by the government for welfare or other purposes with the money proceeds of the government bonds financed by bank credit expansion.

In the absence of the gold standard, there is no way to protect savings from confiscation through inflation. There is no safe store of value. If there were, the government would have to make its holding illegal, as was done in the case of gold. If everyone decided, for example, to convert all his bank deposits to silver or copper or any other good, and thereafter declined to accept checks as payment for goods, bank deposits would lose their purchasing power and government-created bank credit would be worthless as a claim on goods. The financial policy of the welfare state requires that there be no way for the owners of wealth to protect themselves.

This is the shabby secret of the welfare statists' tirades against gold. Deficit spending is simply a scheme for the "hidden" confiscation of wealth. Gold stands in the way of this insidious process. It stands as a protector of property rights. If one grasps this, one has no difficulty in understanding the statists' antagonism toward the gold standard.[1]

Since political freedom requires economic freedom and gold and economic freedom are inseparable, it becomes clear why the gold standard has been a point of contention between free enterprisers and socialists.

The gold standard is a monetary system and a regulating device, a feedback mechanism which acts as a regulator to maintain a certain balance. The more play allowed in such a mechanism, the more the balance is jeopardized. Thus, after World War I, the brake exerted by the gold standard had been, if not removed, considerably loosened. Once play was allowed, it became possible to surrender to the great tide of prosperity and inflation. The day the snag occurred, it was necessary to go as far down the road of depression as one had advanced on that of credit expansion. Black Friday, 1929, gave the first warning of the impending crisis which in successive waves was to spread throughout the United States and to every country in Europe. The Great Depression should have signaled that something was basically wrong with a system that permits such *a* catastrophe to occur at all. [2]

In Rep. Paul's recent conversations with Alan Greenspan, Greenspan said the central bankers had become smart enough to achieve all the benefits of the gold standard without its limitations. The record of the 1990s and the current meltdown indicate otherwise, and Greenspan still supports his conclusion that in the absence of the gold standard, there is no way to protect savings from confiscation through inflation. Although he still recognizes the danger of excessive credit, he inflated the currency endlessly during his tenure. The gold standard eliminates the risk of human error between theory and application.

A free functioning gold standard brings things back into balance and will not cease until equilibrium is restored. The gold standard governs domestic and international transactions with faultless effectiveness. Capitalism and the gold standard tend to maintain the perpetuation of a free economic system. While the gold standard guides men's actions, it respects their freedom of choice.[3]

14

THREE VARIATIONS OF THE GOLD STANDARD

Originally the true gold standard, sometimes called the orthodox, classical or pure gold standard, was a "gold-coin standard." All paper money was backed one hundred per cent by gold and convertible into gold. Gold coins were actually in the cash holdings of the people, in addition to bank notes, checkbook money, and fractional coins. Paper was a money substitute payable on demand in gold coins. From 1882 to 1933 the United States' currency was backed by gold coins. They were called "gold certificates"; the color of the back of the paper note was gold and at the bottom of the obverse side it said, "United States of America, Fifty Dollars, In Gold Coin Payable To The Bearer On Demand." Since they were redeemable into gold, they represented definite quantities of the metal gold. Both gold coins and paper notes, money substitutes, were in circulation. Under the gold-coin standard, money was gold and gold was money.

Since the beginning of the 20th century, however, governments have undermined the gold standard. From the gold-coin standard, where the people had actual possession of gold coins as the circulating medium of exchange, governments gradually established the "gold-bullion standard," which afforded greater leeway for inflation and familiarized the people with paper money. The people innocently trusted the paper which was theoretically, but not in practice, as good as gold. Under this standard the government managed the gold bullion. Since gold coins were confiscated in the United States in 1933, they were no longer in circulation, and were accumulated in the vaults of central banks. The national currency was no longer redeemable in gold coins by United States citizens, but convertibility was retained between governments.

The gold standard was further eroded by the "gold-exchange standard." Governments began holding their country's gold reserves not in actual gold, but in foreign claims to gold, i.e., dollars and pounds were redeemable in gold, so central banks held paper dollars and paper pounds that were supposedly "as good as gold." By making only two currencies redeemable in gold, the world's monetary gold was gradually accumulated in a few central banks, which eventually became the reserve banks of the world.

After World War II the Bank of England and the United States Federal Reserve System controlled most of the world's stock of monetary gold; the United States controlled almost $24.5 billion in gold out of total $40 billion gold. More than sixty nations, forming the sterling area, held their reserves in pound sterling claims to gold. Twenty nations, mainly in Latin America, constituted the dollar area. The Bank of England, in turn, held most of its reserves in dollar claims to gold, making the Federal Reserve System the ultimate reserve bank of the world. Thus, the international gold-exchange standard was reduced to a "de facto" dollar-exchange standard.

During the 1960s, the decade of the New Frontier and the Great Society, social programs were being paid by the mushrooming money supply of the United States. The dollar slowly fell from its position of predominance. Several monetary crises and runs on the British pound triggered worldwide demands for dollar redemption, greatly depleting the gold reserves of the United States and thus creating precarious payment situations. In 1968, the United States gold supply stood at approximately $11 billion, while foreigners held over 35 billion dollars "convertible" into gold. The next step signaled the end was near. In March, 1968, most governments joined the United States and put an embargo on gold payments and halted gold redemption of their currencies. This act was essentially a declaration of bankruptcy of the United States Treasury, the international monetary "dollar-exchange standard," and, of all the individual currencies which took part in this gold-dollar scheme. This was the end of the gold-exchange standard and the beginning of the "fiat standard," which is no standard at all.

Although the gold standard produced price stability for 146 years and the period of the greatest economic growth of any nation in the history of the world, this price stability was an obstacle to government expansion and profiteering by those corporations aligned with government. The gold standard was under continual attack until 1933, when it succumbed to government intervention leading to its eventual abolishment. From 1933 onward, Americans, and from 1968 onward, foreigners, have been plagued with endless inflation.

Purchasing Power of the Dollar

(1792 = 1.00)

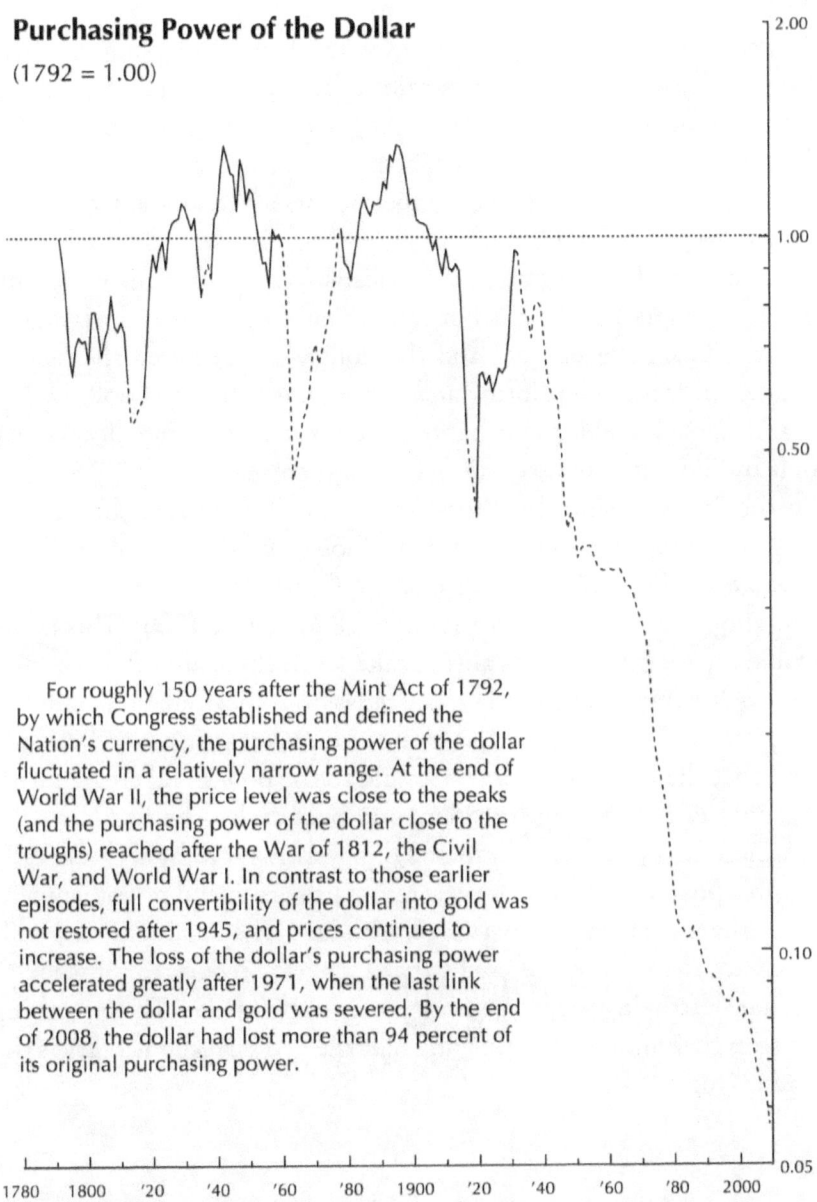

For roughly 150 years after the Mint Act of 1792, by which Congress established and defined the Nation's currency, the purchasing power of the dollar fluctuated in a relatively narrow range. At the end of World War II, the price level was close to the peaks (and the purchasing power of the dollar close to the troughs) reached after the War of 1812, the Civil War, and World War I. In contrast to those earlier episodes, full convertibility of the dollar into gold was not restored after 1945, and prices continued to increase. The loss of the dollar's purchasing power accelerated greatly after 1971, when the last link between the dollar and gold was severed. By the end of 2008, the dollar had lost more than 94 percent of its original purchasing power.

Note: Purchasing power was calculated from the Wholesale Price Index (source: Bureau of Labor Statistics, U.S. Department of Labor). The broken portions of the curve are periods when redeemability of the dollar into the monetary commodities at fixed rates was suspended.

In 1968, the gates were flung wide open for worldwide inflation. Governments were going to play it "deuces wild." From that point on there has been no legal or procedural restraint of any kind, domestically or internationally, on the printing and spending of paper dollars by the United States government—nor on the paper money printing and spending of any other government that accepts paper dollars as "reserve assets"—that were once, as good as gold.

Although gold ownership by Americans was legalized as of December 31, 1974, paper money was not redeemable in gold. The government severed the link between gold and the dollar. This allowed the federal government to continue printing and monetizing billions of dollars. The Federal Reserve was able to push interest rates so low that credit was easy to come by and big businesses freely helped themselves.

In the 35 years since this book was originally written, the government's gross debt has risen from $380.9 billion in 1970, 37.6% of the GDP, to $9,985.8 trillion in 2008, 70.2% of the GDP. Estimates of the gross debt total by 2010 are $14,456.3 trillion, 98.1% of the GDP. This is the inevitable course governments always take when there are no checks and balances on their spending. After every inflation comes deflation, or in our case, a depression and contraction of the economy starting in 2007. Keep in mind that the Federal Reserve was sold to the public and created with the purpose of eliminating the boom and bust cycle. The Fed lacks the checks and balances of other branches of government to hold to a fiscally responsible position. Thus we see the temptation to spend by government is greater than its promise to balance the budget. The Fed is only too willing to create the money and credit that Congress requests even though inflation is destroying the purchasing power of the dollar. The only thing able to stop government spending and halt the Fed's irresponsibility is the gold standard.

15

INFLATION OR THE GOLD STANDARD

The politicians were quick to take advantage of their newfound spending power—a power that allowed them to increase government spending (usually popular) without increasing taxes (always unpopular). Although there were no legal limits to the United States government's deficit spending, there remained one economic limit, a remnant of the gold standard. There existed a domestic tie between the dollar and gold—a "legal requirement" that the Federal Reserve "maintain" gold reserves against its notes and other liabilities with no domestic obligation to pay them out. Politicians being politicians overcame the obstacle.

For 140 years, prior to 1934, the United States dollar was an honored promise to "pay on demand" .77 ounces of silver or .05 ounces (1/20th ounce) of gold, a ratio of sixteen to one. The plain language of the Constitution defines "lawful money" as gold or silver and *prohibits any governmental body from naming anything else money*. It assigned only a restricted power to Congress to "regulate the value" of the dollar, i.e., to change the definition of its weight in silver or gold. In 1934, following a ten-month gold embargo, President Roosevelt by edict, Executive Order 6102, changed the value of the dollar in gold to .028 ounces (1/35th ounce) from .05 ounces. He left the value in silver unchanged at .77 ounces, creating a new silver/gold monetary ratio of twenty-seven to one from sixteen to one.

At the same time as this first "devaluation" of the dollar, Congress passed the Gold Reserve Act of 1934. It terminated circulation of gold coins and free convertibility of the paper currency into gold for United States citizens and prohibited them from holding gold (except rare coins) in the United States. A prohibition President Eisenhower extended in the 1950s to holding gold abroad. The only remaining domestic link between the dollar and gold was an inconsequential carry-over from early days—a requirement that the Federal Reserve maintain gold reserves against its notes and other liabilities.

Initially, in the 1930s, the requirement set these reserves at forty per cent against notes and thirty-five percent against other liabilities. In practice, the legal reserve requirement was quite meaningless. Each time the paper money supply was inflated to the legal limit, the legal minimum reserve limit was reduced. In 1945, the reserve requirement was reduced to twenty-five per cent on both notes and liabilities. In 1965, the reserve requirement against liabilities was abolished. In 1968, the twenty-five per cent gold reserve requirement against Federal Reserve notes in circulation was dropped by an act of Congress. The last legal restraint on the unlimited printing of paper dollars was removed.

> Removal of the gold reserve requirement for Federal Reserve notes (your paper money) eliminated the last barrier to inflating continually the Nation's purchasing media. As long as a substantial gold reserve was required by law, the money-credit managers were confronted with a restraining influence.
>
> Now, only the wisdom and determination of the Nation's money-credit managers can prevent the ultimate decline of the buying power of the dollar until it becomes worthless. To what extent the citizens can rely on the wisdom and courage of those "responsible men" can be judged by events of the past three decades, including loss of two-thirds of the buying power of savings and life insurance, the increasing rate of depreciation in recent years, loss of much of the Nation's gold, and the fact that several of those managers have been among the most persistent in advocating the removal of all restraints. Truly wise and responsible men would not want to be without the guidance of such an objective criterion as a gold reserve requirement; and unwise, irresponsible men should not be relied upon to act properly without such guidance.
> Judging by the foregoing, the dollar appears doomed to continue losing buying power, the only question being: How long before it will be practically worthless?[1]

No currency in history has lasted more than forty-two years after its intrinsic value has been abandoned.[2]

The runaway deficit spending by the United States government in the 1960s created runaway inflation in the 1970s. The "federal debt" in 1960 was $290.9 billion; by 1970 it was $382.6 billion. That is a $91.7 billion or a thirty-one per cent increase in the federal debt in only ten years. Federal tax revenues in the seven years from 1965 to 1972 increased sixty-eight per cent from $117 billion to $198 billion, while in the same period, outlays soared one hundred per cent, from $118 billion to $236 billion.[1]

Today, the 1970 debt of $382.6 billion seems insignificant compared to 2008's debt of $9,985.8 trillion. How easily we've become used to this insidious process. It is easy to complain about higher prices, but it requires more effort to see the connection.

The politicians acted quickly upon their ill-gotten spending power. The two to three per cent inflation of the early sixties accelerated to five to six per cent inflation in the late sixties, and the seventies were faced with nine to ten per cent inflation. At ten per cent annual inflation, the currency depreciates one hundred per cent every ten years or prices double every ten years, or less.

The effects of inflation on the fixed income group of retired people, those on annuities, pensions, or social security, and the poor, are inhuman. It is impossible to plan for retirement under such circumstances. As of 2009, many retirees are being forced to work because they can't afford to retire. This is the future which socialist paper money advocates have arranged for every citizen. A life of productive work is rewarded with an old age of poverty through degraded currency and purchasing power. Inflation is cruel, inhuman, and barbaric.

Must inflation always exist, embezzling the individual's hard-earned money, savings, and plans for the future? No!

Socialist governments are eager to stay in power, to spend other people's money, to rob Peter to pay Paul, to think up non-profitable schemes that waste the taxpayer's money and always pretend to know what is best. Socialists of all persuasions have systematically sabotaged and destroyed the only objective standard and protection the individual has for his earnings and savings. The gold standard did not fail—it was assassinated.

Under the gold standard, inflationary policies are not impossible, but made difficult. The gold standard is not a perfect or ideal standard. Ludwig von Mises points out that nobody is in a position to dictate how something more satisfactory could be put in place of the gold standard. Only the market can be trusted to determine the best currency.

The gold standard means sound money; it makes the value of money independent of government. The purchasing power of the gold is unstable. But the idea of absolute stability and un-changeability of purchasing power is absurd. In a living, changing world there can be no such thing as stability of purchasing power. It is an essential feature of money that its purchasing power changes with market demands. The adversaries of the gold standard do not want to make money's purchasing power stable; they want government to have the power to manipulate purchasing power, i.e., wages, prices, and interest rates, without being hindered by the will of the consumer.

Socialists' main objection to the gold standard is that the determination of prices is out of the government's control. There is an "external" or "automatic" force that restrains governments monetary power—the vicissitudes of gold production. Since the production of gold depends on its profitability, like all commodities, the significance of the gold standard is the supply of gold limits the government's power preventing inflation. The gold standard makes the purchasing power of money independent of the ambitions, whims, and doctrines of political parties and special interest groups. The limits are not a defect of the gold standard; they are its main excellence.

Every method of manipulating purchasing power is by necessity arbitrary and harmful to the market. For example, if government forces prices above the market level, surpluses result; if government forces prices below the market level, shortages result; if government forces prices to remain at the market level, its function is superfluous. The gold standard removes from government control the power to tamper with money's purchasing power.

To accept this concept, one must acknowledge that government cannot make all the people richer by printing money. The abhorrence of the gold standard is inspired by the superstition that omnipotent governments can create wealth out of little scraps of paper. The gold standard cannot totally stop inflation, but it can check large-scale destructive inflationary ventures. It can prove a safe haven for one's money while paper depreciates.

The gold standard protects the monetary system from the influence of government. Metallic money is not subject to government manipulation. The gold standard is an efficacious check upon credit expansion, as it forces the banks not to exceed certain limits in their expansionist ventures. Unconditional redemption keeps currencies at par with gold. The gold standard's own inflationary potentialities are kept within limits by the supply and demand of gold in the free market and the the profitability of gold mining.

Under the gold standard, gold is money and money is gold, and the values of both are determined by the consumers' buying or abstention from buying on the free market.

Under capitalism, the government has only one monetary objective: to facilitate and to simplify the use of the medium of exchange which the people through the market have chosen as money. Since a nation's currency should be sound, gold or silver coins should be properly assayed and the bars of bullion coined in a way to make the detection of clipping, abrasion, and counterfeiting easy. To the government's stamp no function is attributed other than to certify the weight and the fineness of the metal contained, although private enterprise can do it cheaper. Debased or worn coins are taken out of circulation and re-minted. The market for money should be free and competitive.

During the California gold rush, private mints were established whose honesty and integrity were undeniable. Coins of those early private mints today are selling at substantial premiums and are some of the most prized specimens of notable coin collectors.

Since the abandonment of the gold standard, the quantity of currency held by the public between 1933 and 1972 rose from $5.5 billion to $66.6 billion, demand deposits from $13.5 billion to $178.6 billion, and time deposits from $21.8 billion to $309.3 billion. As of August 2009, public currency held is $856 billion, demand deposits are $476 billion, and time deposits, as of 2006 when it was discontinued, are $1,400 trillion (Board of Governors of FRS, ALFRED series). During this period the dollar's purchasing power has fallen to pennies of the 1933 dollar. This is the result of government's inflation. A dollar in 1913 is worth .05 today, or it cost $21 to buy what a 1913 dollar bought.

Although inflation is a vicious form of taxation, it is popular to big government, big corporations and big bankers because its effects are rarely understood. The beneficiaries of inflation sing loud praises of "easy money" and "credit expansion." The government and its economists invent intricate theories and doctrines to support their inflationary policies. Inflation temporarily boosts government revenue and permits politicians to spend more than they can raise by taxes. Inflation, as it dilutes the value of the money, repudiates government debt, at the expense of every working man.

In this respect, it is a silent tax on innocent currency holders and savers. If the circumstances were clearly laid before the taxpayers, government would have no chance obtaining the consent of the people to support its wars and bail out programs of large corporations and banks, which should be allowed to go bankrupt.

War, in particular, requires inflation. Financing wars by bank paper hides the true cost from the voter. To fight a war is extremely costly. Under the gold standard, the costs are apparent to the people and they are reluctant to incur such vast expenses. Wars are now financed through subterfuge and inflation. If America had remained on the gold standard, it is unlikely it would have been involved in most of the wars it has fought since W.W. II.

Financing war by paper money creates large profits for banks and the military-industrial complex. Bankers constitute a powerful vested interest in favor of war, where they can create paper money in vast sums to lend to needy governments. Bankers conspire to bring about wars by influencing foreign policy. The last century with central banking was also the century of total war. The Fed was created in 1913. The stock of money started to rise in 1914. By 1920 it was double the 1914 level, when the Fed opened for business. We entered W.W. I in 1918 with only 21 percent of the war funded through taxation. The remainder was funded by Fed-backed borrowing (56%) and outright money creation (23%), for a total cost of $33 billion. The country has become a killing machine.

Few people understand the losses which inflation inflicts on millions of people. Inflation breeds a political and economic radicalism that tends to destroy the private property order. After great inflations Lenin, Hitler and Mao came to power. The nationalizing schemes used by former President Bush and current President Obama are similar grabs for power.

Hitler succeeded in coming to terms with inflation. He understood that inflation destroys the ties which bind men to reality and threatens freedom and the social order. To save the social order, he sacrificed freedom. By subjecting individual conduct to strict control, he restrained people from utilizing their purchasing power which exceeded the value of purchasable wealth. In this way he was able to distribute generously the means of buying goods which did not exist. He turned this lie into a system of government.

Germany covered her financial deficits by creating paper money and relying upon exceptionally severe controls to keep prices from rising, as well as extended rationing to curb the excess purchasing power created by the deficit. All Germans were supplied with plenty of money, but were kept from spending it by draconian penalties—including the death sentence —which enforced rationing. Hitler's experience with inflation was the natural outcome of economic tyranny. Such tyranny has always resulted in the extinction of individual freedom. Rome had Diocletian. Germany had Hitler. America has the Federal Reserve and Congress.

America was founded on freedom, but it is doomed to disappear unless it manages to break out of the inflationary whirlpool where it is sinking relentlessly before our eyes. Whoever tolerates inflation is a protagonist of dictatorship.[4]

The capitalistic economy can only bear fruit under conditions of stability. If it is to continue functioning it must rest again on the firm monetary basis upon which it was erected. Today after 75 years of inflation, freedom can only be saved by the rehabilitation of our money.

The solution is simple: government should stop inflating. Since the solution seems impossible for government, the gold standard must be employed to clean up the polluted money supply. As Henry Hazlitt observed, gold means trust. It weighs more and can be kept longer than a politician's pledge. Nothing has more clearly demonstrated the need for the gold standard than its abandonment, as the world has been plunged into a sea of paper money, unending inflation and wars.

16

DEPRESSION OR THE GOLD STANDARD

As soon as the inflation and credit expansion stop, the piper (debtor) must be paid. The inevitable readjustments liquidate the unsound investments of the boom. Inflation always leads to depression.

The correct but incomplete theory of depressions and the business cycle began with the eighteenth-century Scottish philosopher and economist David Hume. The work was continued by the eminent nineteenth-century English classical economist David Ricardo. The entire boom and bust theory, however, was not fully developed until the 1920s. The full explanation of the business cycle was developed by Ludwig von Mises in his monumental work, *Theory of Money & Credit*, published in 1912, and nearly a hundred years later still the best book on the theory of money and banking. By 1930, the great dean of monetary theory had discovered the complete phenomenon of the business cycle and the greatness of laissez-faire capitalism.

Business cycles are natural phenomena in the free market. They originate from the functioning of supply and demand factors of products or commodities. Take gold, for example, if the supply is inadequate, the resulting shortage causes the price to rise. As the price rises, the mining of gold becomes more profitable and production increases. The higher the profit the more gold produced. Production continues until it becomes unprofitable to mine more gold. This occurs when supply equals demand. The miners continue producing gold as supply overtakes demand. As demand subsides due to the excess supply, the price falls. If and to the extent production continues the price falls further. When the price has dropped to the level at which the production of more gold is unprofitable, production stops. Smart businessmen slow down their production as the price is falling, others go bankrupt. Production is curtailed to meet the lower demand.

Eventually the low production rate causes a shortage, forces up the price making production profitable and the cycle begins again.

One of the beliefs today in economics, held both by private and government economists, is that the Fed has eliminated the business cycle. This is false. As long as the means of production remain in the private sector and are based on the profit motive, there will be business cycles. An inherent feature of capitalism is that it is unstable. There is a continuous tendency for prices to move in one direction or another. The market is always seeking equilibrium, where supply equals demand, but changes of data, as in consumers changing their demands or technology improving production are always taking place, preventing equilibrium from ever being reached.

These business cycles, of which thousands exist, form an overall cycle. The overall cyclical behavior of an economy is the consequence of the combination and interaction of many small, interdependent cycles. This general economic cycle is known as the "boom and bust cycle."

Prior to World War I the boom and bust cycles were sharp and short-lived. Only certain segments of the economy were hit and only on a short-term basis. The health of the whole economy was never in danger. A main reason for the milder cycles in the nineteenth century was that America was relatively free from government interference. Government respected the efficacy of the free market.

In the nineteenth century, when the businessman-entrepreneur made an investment decision, he was spared the trouble of considering tax consequences, unions, consumer protectionists, ecologists, and government bureaucrats. His entrepreneurial function rested solely on his judgment of whether or not his investment would be profitable. The better his judgment, the higher the profits he earned. If his judgment overestimated the demand for his product, he would suffer losses, and be forced to change or soon be out of business.

The market economy is a profit and loss economy. The intelligence and ability of business entrepreneurs are gauged by the profits and losses they reap. The market contains a built-in mechanism to insure the survival and flourishing of the most productive businessmen and the weeding out of the unproductive ones. The more profits reaped by the successful businessmen, the more they have available to reinvest and the greater their business responsibilities. A few years of making losses drive the unsuccessful entrepreneurs out of business (if government doesn't bail them out).

This profit and loss mechanism tends to keep businesses in the black and business failures at a minimum.

The business cycle is not capable of producing the severe inflation-depression cycle known in modern times. The inflation-depression cycle is a result of interference in the money market by the Fed and the banking industry. Together they have the capacity to expand credit and the money supply—first, in the form of paper money or bank notes, and later in the form of demand deposits or checking accounts, which are instantly redeemable in cash at the banks. The operations of commercial banks are key to the extreme movements of the boom and bust cycle, which had puzzled observers since the mid-eighteenth century.

Dr. Murray Rothbard[1] explains how the boom and bust cycle gets its disruptive power from the banking system. The natural moneys, gold and silver, are useful commodities. If money were confined to these commodities, then the economy would work in the aggregate, as it does in particular markets. There would be a smooth adjustment of supply and demand and, therefore, no boom and bust cycles. But the injection of bank credit adds a crucial and disruptive element.

Even though the money is backed by gold, banks can expand credit in the form of notes or deposits which are theoretically redeemable on demand in gold, but in practice are not. For example, if a bank has 1,000 ounces of gold in its vault and it issues instantly redeemable receipts for 2,500 ounces of gold, and if there were no concerted pressure for redemption, the bank has been able to expand the money supply by 1,500 gold ounces.

The banks continue to expand credit, for the more they expand credit the greater their profits. As the money supply increases it bids up prices. The result is inflation and a boom within the country. The citizens naturally start to buy more goods from other countries where prices are lower. And foreigners buy fewer goods in the inflated country. The results are trade and balance of payments deficits. By imports exceeding exports, money flows to foreign countries.

Foreigners, having no need for foreign paper money, present the money for redemption in gold. Thus gold is the money that flows persistently out of a country which has inflation. During this period the banks have continued inflating, placing perhaps 4,000 ounces of gold receipts in circulation while the gold base has dwindled to, say, 800. Eventually the banks lose their nerve because they are obligated to redeem those notes. In order to save themselves, they stop their credit expansion and their outstanding bank loans contract.

The bank contraction reverses the boom and the bust follows. The fall in the supply of bank money leads to a general fall in prices. Goods become cheaper and competitive again. The balance of payments reverses itself and gold flows back into the country. As bank money contracts on top of an expanding gold base, the condition of the banks again becomes sound.

This natural readjustment by the markets is the depression phase of the business cycle. It is the preceding inflation that makes the depression phase necessary. The depression is the process by which the economy throws off the excesses of the boom and reestablishes a sound economic condition. When the banks are in a confident position to resume their natural path of credit expansion, the cycle repeats itself.

The point here is that the boom-bust cycle is brought about, not by the free market, but by the fractional reserve banking system. The banks can only expand in unison when a central bank exists. The central bank is a privileged position imposed by government monopoly over the entire banking system. If banks were truly competitive, any credit expansion by one bank would quickly pile up the debts of that bank in its competitors, who would quickly call for redemption. In short, a bank's rivals will call upon it for redemption in gold or cash in the same way as do foreigners. With domestic banks the process is much faster and would nip any incipient inflation in the bud.

By systematic intervention, government is the ultimate cause of bank expansion and inflation. When inflation comes to an end, the subsequent depression-readjustment comes into play. Without bank credit expansion, supply and demand tend toward equilibrium through the free price system; no cumulative booms and busts can develop.

The Fed sets artificially low interest rates and pours cheap new loan funds into the business community triggering another disruptive element which eventually collapses the entire economy. The interest rate in the free market is artificially lowered by the Fed, causing the eventual and sudden cluster of business failures and the capital goods market to be hit harder than the consumer goods market.

A brief breakdown follows. Businessmen, seeing the rate of interest fall, assume the public is saving and investing more money. They react as they always would and must to such a change of market signals: they expand their investment in durable equipment, in capital goods, in industrial raw material, in construction, as compared to their direct production of consumer goods. In short, businessmen react as if savings had genuinely increased and they happily borrow the cheap and abundant money.

As they invest in capital goods—machines, equipment, industrial plants—the money filters through the economy and wages and prices are bid up. The inflationary boom continues as long as money remains cheap. The longer it continues the wider the distortions of the pricing and production system.

When the banks get into a shaky condition as they did in 2007, the bank credit expansion finally stops and the excesses start to surface. Two years later, we are still seeing the destructive results of the artificially low interest rates. Investors have lost billions of dollars. Through the recession, the consumers reestablish their consumption/investment ratio. It is then revealed that business had invested too much in capital goods and had underinvested in consumer goods. The prices of labor and raw materials in the capital goods market had been bid up during the boom too high to be profitable. Business had been tricked, by the government's monetary policy into thinking more savings were available to invest than were really there.

The "depression" is then seen as the necessary and healthy phase by which the market liquidates the unsound, unprofitable investments of the boom, and reestablishes the consumption/investment ratio actually desired by the people, the consumers. The depression is painful, but necessary. The prices of labor and goods in the capital goods industries must be allowed to fall until proper supply and demand relations are resumed.

According to Mises, the blame rests on the inflationary bank credit expansion propelled by the intervention of government and its central bank. The solution is government must stop inflating.

The longer the government waits to stop the inflation, the worse the necessary readjustments will have to be. The Fed has kept interest rates artificially low for years rather than allowing the market to adjust. Hence, the current recession of 2008-9 is more severe and lasting longer than necessary.

The government must never try to prop up or lend money to unsound businesses and reinflate as it is doing today. Propping up unsound businesses will prolong the agony and convert a sharp, quick depression phase into a lingering and chronic disease, resulting in mass unemployment. The government must do nothing to encourage consumption; it must not increase its own expenditures, for this will further distort the social consumption/investment ratio. In fact, cutting the government budget and expenses will improve the ratio. The economy doesn't need more consumption spending, but more saving in order to validate some of the excessive investments of the boom.

The Misesian solution is the exact opposite of the Keynesian: Government keeps absolute hands off the economy, and to confine itself to stopping its own inflation and to cutting its own budget.[2]

To sum up, whenever a free market economy exists, business cycles will occur. Business cycles are part of the normal functioning of supply and demand. It is the business cycle that renders the free market the most efficient means of satisfying consumer demands.

When the business cycle corrects itself, it is the natural process by which it throws off the excesses of the previous "boom" cycle. Since there are thousands of products in the marketplace, there are thousands of cycles. Since cycles run independently and at different lengths to each other, some are booming while others are busting. This keeps the economy on a steady path of progress. There is never any danger of upsetting the entire economy.

When government tampers with the market, it upsets the natural balance of the business cycle. By artificially increasing the supply of money or expanding credit, it stimulates the entire economy with its cheap money policy. When the liquidating depression takes over it spreads throughout the business world, causing the entire economy to collapse.

According to Mises, during a depression or recession the government should step out of the picture and let market forces straighten out the mess. This way the depression is quick and sharp allowing the economy to get back to the business of business. Government by nature is meddlesome. It converts a short, healthy recession into a lingering and chronic depression. Today, the subprime housing market is reflecting the entire subprime economic system, which is due to artificially low interest rates.

This was the story of the Great Depression of the 1930s. The Depression was not a result of capitalism which socialists are so eager to accuse. The 1929 crash was made inevitable by the vast inflationary policies of the Western governments and their central banks during the 1920s. A policy deliberately adopted by all Western governments, including the Federal Reserve. The depression that followed the crash was also inevitable. Its long duration was not. The deliberately adopted programs and government meddling kept the economy in a constant state of uncertainty and confusion. Market forces could not right themselves. Government interference prolonged the depression. For the first time in American history, there existed a nearly perpetual depression and nearly permanent mass unemployment due to unprecedented government intervention.

The debacle of the Great Depression was a result of the failure of Western governments to return to the gold standard after W. W. I.

The gold standard would have deflated most postwar economies, especially England's. Instead, the "gold-exchange standard" was adopted. The gold-exchange standard enabled countries to back their currency not only with gold, but with dollars or sterling, paper money, which was supposedly convertible into gold. The gold-exchange standard worked in such a way that when money left one country it added purchasing power to the second country, while leaving the purchasing power of the first country intact, creating a duplication of purchasing power. Since capital flowed without gold payments following, the gold-exchange standard postponed the simple correction the gold standard would have realized. Consequently, the gold-exchange standard was one of the main causes of the inflationary boom that lasted until 1929, when the day of reckoning came.

Every experience with irredeemable paper money in America's history has failed. The government's malicious inflationary action is demolishing the hard work of American industry. Every scheme with cheap money has hurt the public welfare. The cost has been more than a purely specie currency would have cost if each generation had had to buy it anew.

To paraphrase Professor William Graham Sumner, the great Yale economist of the pre-Federal Reserve era, a new gold-coin standard could be established every year out of the depreciation losses suffered by the millions of honest productive men in society. The needed gold could be purchased again and again from the losses suffered by the millions of victims of a depression. Indeed, the gold-coin standard is a bargain price for economic stability.[3]

17

FALLACIES ABOUT THE GOLD STANDARD

Some people trust in the efficacy of the gold standard, but argue against its establishment. They believe it is irrational, immoral, or impractical. There are ten main fallacies about the gold standard that prevent Americans from giving it the support it deserves. Once these fallacious beliefs are eliminated by reason, logic, and facts, support of the gold standard can spread nationwide, even worldwide.

The first fallacy is that gold is mystical; people are drawn to gold because of some mysterious, irrational, irresistible charm. And if governments did not use gold for monetary purposes the price of gold would be much less than it is. In reality, when the United States closed the gold window in August, 1971, gold was selling around $43 an ounce. One year later it sold for $65 an ounce, a fifty per cent increase. Two years later it sold for $120 an ounce. By 1980 gold sold for $800 an ounce. When governments prohibit the individual's choice to own gold, gold sells at a premium. When governments respect the individual's choice, the price of gold stabilizes and the premium disappears.

People are attracted to gold for very good reasons. It has many uses in industry, and as money, it is par excellence. Those who see no value in gold are blind to reason. Gold is not mystical. The real mystical idea is that by proclaiming the magic words "legal tender," Congress can make a worthless piece of paper and ink into a thing of value. The ideas of something for nothing and that wealth can be created by printing pieces of paper, are mystical. Only a "legal tender" law passed and enforced by a government can make a two and a half inch by six inch piece of United States currency, whose industrial value is a small fraction of a cent, acquire a value of one dollar or a hundred dollars.

Gold is real; it has objective value to people, and its market value is determined by free exchange, not by the pronouncement of a government via a mystical procedure unknown to the general public.[1]

The second fallacy is that the gold standard is old-fashioned. Because something has been effective for a long period of time does not make it old-fashioned. It is its dependability that necessitates its perpetuation. To the extent man requires a code of values to guide his thoughts and actions; he requires a standard of value to guide his monetary judgments. Inalienable rights and unchanging principles such as those of the Founding Fathers' are not old-fashioned. "Good" and "right" are always fashionable. The value of money should always be kept stable, backed by the honesty and integrity, i.e., the gold reserves of the government or the bank issuing the money. In the words of Jacques Rueff, the famous French economist, "Tomorrow, to save man, we will give him a real currency."[1]

The third fallacy is that the gold standard is severe and inhuman. Just the opposite is true. Paper money and inflation oppress the poor. Paper money robs the poor and middle classes. Daniel Webster, in 1832 on the floor of Congress denounced printing press money as the deceit it is.

> Of all the contrivances for cheating the laboring classes of mankind, none have been more effectual than that which deludes them with paper money. This is the most effectual of inventions to fertilize the rich man's field by the sweat of the poor man's brow. Ordinary tyranny, oppression, excessive taxation . . . these bear lightly on the happiness of the mass of the community compared with fraudulent currencies and the robberies committed by depreciated paper.

It is unlimited paper money that yields huge profits to banks who issue endless amounts of credit. The losers are the rest of the community because the created money claims real goods, which are bid up in price or no longer available to the community which produced them in the first place. The gold standard stands in the way of this insidious process. It serves justice and humanity.

The fourth fallacy is the idea that gold can be replaced by "paper gold" or Special Drawing Rights (SDRs). This concept is the invention of Keynesian economists, who believe abstract ideas are more important than reality. Since real gold is scarce and expensive, their ideal is paper gold. Their idea of gold is an abstraction, and abstractions can be created out of nothing. As Donald J. Hoppe points out, there is one difficulty: abstract ideas are like soap bubbles; when they are touched they disappear. SDRs are based on the same abstraction as the fiat money of the United

States—Federal Reserve notes. Although SDRs are defined in terms of gold they can never actually be redeemed in gold.

> They are intended forever to remain abstractions—evidences of debt that can never be repaid. Money is to be debt and debt is to be credit, and the debt is evidenced by interest-bearing notes or bonds. When due, the principle and the interest on the bonds are paid from the proceeds raised by the sale of more bonds. The more we get into debt the richer we are to become.[3]

This is the theory of paper gold. It is the most mystical and irrational of all ideas. The government can force its citizens to accept inconvertible and worthless paper money, but it cannot force other nations to accept it. The world needs no more paper; it needs more stability—gold.

The fifth fallacy is that an increase in the price of gold would benefit only those countries mining it. The United States shipped millions of dollars worth of surface gold mining machinery to Russia through San Francisco under the Lend-Lease program after the closing of most of the gold mines in the United States in 1942.[2] This enabled Russia to boost her gold mining production and at the same time end gold production in the United States. A rise in gold price would make gold mining profitable in the United States, increasing gold production at home while saving individual freedom. Increasing gold production would make gold money available, and reverse the nation's trend toward socialism and self-destruction. On balance, the United States would benefit most.

Fallacy number six is that in a major crisis the gold standard "breaks down." The example usually cited is that after World War I, when Great Britain returned to the gold standard, she had to abandon it six years later. The problem was that Britain suffered from wartime inflation; prices in Britain in 1924 were seventy per cent above their prewar level. But the British government decided to resume the gold standard, in 1925, at the prewar and pre-inflation parity. The British were unwilling to make corresponding cuts in retail prices and wage rates, which would cut prices to the prewar level, the result was falling exports, stagnation, and unemployment. It was the gold standard itself, not the false rate or internal flexibility of set wages that got the blame.

What Britain and most governments wanted the gold standard to do was prop up their ailing currencies, retain the old parity rate, and prevent the devaluation that was required by the wartime inflation. They said their currencies were as good as gold and rendered inflation as invisible as the emperor's new clothes. But the public knew the truth. The currencies were heavily inflated beyond their gold reserves. The government should have allowed gold to seek its own free market level and then resume convertibility of the sterling. Although this would have resulted in a devaluation of the pound, though economically correct, politically unpalatable. The result was a steady fall in wholesale prices from 1925 until September, 1931, when Britain abandoned the gold standard. It was the United States "helping" Britain retain the false prewar rate of $4.86 instead of insisting the actual devalued rate that had sunk as low as $3.18 in February, 1920, that caused the Great Depression of the 1930s around the world, and forced the abandonment of the gold standard by the United States in 1933. The gold standard did not break down; it was deliberately destroyed along with the economies of the civilized world.

Fallacy number seven is the idea that the "fiat standard" is more workable than the "gold standard." "Fiat" is a polite word for "worthless." Worthless money can only work for planners and bureaucrats; it lets the public servant become the master. The fiat standard, via inflation, is the means by which governments expand and gain control of the people and their property. The debt standard sows the seeds of its own destruction. In fact, "From the days of ancient Rome, history reveals that any nation foolish enough to adopt fiat money has suffered an economic collapse, and many such nations have disappeared from the face of the earth. No currency in history has lasted more than 42 years after its intrinsic base has been abandoned."[5] The fiat standard goes with the welfare state; the gold standard goes with the private property state. Worthless money and the welfare state go hand in hand down the path of self-destruction to oblivion. Strong money and the private property state go hand in hand up the path of prosperity, patriotism, and freedom. The gold standard prevents excessive inflation. Its unmanageability is its main excellence.

The eighth fallacy is that gold creates inflation. Socialists claim that raising the price of gold would create inflation. However, the price of gold was frozen in 1934 at $35 an ounce until 1971 and the United States suffered inflation after 1934. Inflation is caused by an increase in the supply of money and credit. It is government-created. Inflation is like a cancer; unless it is completely stopped, it will spread until it eventually kills the entity. Gold is an inflation-fighter. It destroys the cancer and renders the entity fit to live.

In a free market, the quantity of goods and services determines the price and production of gold. This way gold maintains the price stability of all commodities. Indeed, between 1850 and 1900 many prospectors must have wondered if the huge quantity of gold produced would push prices higher. But just the opposite happened; it stimulated world production of all goods. As George Bernard Shaw said, ". . . With a gold currency it tends to maintain itself even when the natural supply of gold is increased by discoveries of new deposits, because of the curious fact that the demand for gold in the world is practically infinite . . ." Furthermore, during the 146 years from the establishment of the gold standard in 1787 until it was abandoned in 1933, the price level remained stable. Wholesale prices in 1787 were approximately the same as they were 146 years later. This remarkable feat was the result of a stable currency and capitalism, which has a tendency toward lowering the price level of commodities. The record shows the gold standard has proven itself in its ability to fight inflation; no other monetary system has.

The ninth fallacy is: digging up gold from one place simply to bury it again in another place is a waste of money and energy. This is partially true. Nevertheless, money managers and central bankers have proven throughout history they cannot be trusted to keep the value of money sound. By its demented economic and fiscal policies of the last seven decades, the United States has forfeited all confidence in its ability to maintain the value of its currency. It is certainly no waste of money and energy to dig up gold and bury it again if that process keeps the paper money sound and inflation a thing of the past. Gold should be dug up to be minted, and spent—put into circulation. Gold is good, hard, instant money--great reasons for minting it.

The tenth and final fallacy about the gold standard is that there is not enough gold available to use it for money. This is also partially true. The gold mines in the United States were forced to shut down in 1942 by Federal Government order No. L-208. This action destroyed the gold mining industry in the United States. Whenever a mine is closed, the tunnels fill with water, the supports rot, and the machinery rusts. The damage inflicted upon the mining industry was tremendous, and to this day, the government has never made an offer to reimburse any of the mine own-ers for the intentional destruction. Another reason for a gold shortage is hoarding. A principle seen true throughout history; whenever people lose confidence in their government and their currency, they hoard the real, hard money—gold. Consequently, gold coins and gold bullion have been hoarded for decades. During unstable economic times, gold hoarding has accelerated as all paper money in the world is suspect.

A revival in gold thinking would reverse this trend, and the confidence it would produce in the public's mind would release this gold from hiding. As in the Byzantine Empire, where gold flowed freely, the United States and the rest of the world would once again be adequately supplied with gold.

A higher gold price is the incentive to find new discoveries. There has even been talk of reclaiming gold from the ocean. But there is plenty of gold closer to home and cheaper to mine in the continental United States, especially in California. According to the Division of Mines, over 20,000 gold mines are closed in California alone. Jack Sheedy, owner of the Telegraph mine in Downieville, California, said, "There is more gold left in California than ever was taken out." In the Mother Lode of California, there are only two mines that go below a mile in depth. The others have never been mined below the 2,500 foot level. Yet the forma-tion is the same. The two deeper mines paid off every foot of the way, and many engineers claim this area alone has the potential of South Africa.[6] In testimony before a House committee a few years ago, some engineers' reports showed only ten per cent of the available gold supply has ever been removed from the earth.

When Captain Leppert was elected President of the Western Mining Council, he made a conscientious effort to do something about reopening the gold mines. Most of the gold mining areas in the United States are economically depressed areas, and the reopening of these mines would require 50,000 miners alone. Since it requires ten workers in other occu-pations to support a gold miner, this would create half a million jobs, and would remove the "depressed area" label from many communities. Captain Leppert discovered something else: "The gold mines in the United States are closed because somebody in Washington wants them closed."[7] This is dangerous to our national security and to the economy. Senator Byrd once said the gold drain, from the U.S. Treasury, was more of a threat to the security of our nation than the atomic bomb. The security of any nation is the number one responsibility of its government. Restoration of the gold standard should be government's number one priority.

Actually, there is more gold per capita now than ever before. The greatest era of gold production in history has occurred thus far in the twentieth century. There are untold billions in gold-ore reserves waiting to be mined, as soon as it becomes profitable to do so. There is more than enough gold to reestablish a full international gold standard, *if it were properly used*, as a balancing wheel for international trade. There is, and always has been enough gold to finance balanced international trade. There will never be enough gold—or anything else—to finance policies of unrestrained deficits.[8]

Today socialism is moving along at a fast pace because too many people in and out of government are demanding that government should guarantee security rather than liberty. In their quest for security via government-subsidized programs in education, agriculture, healthcare, insurance, automobiles, and so on, liberty is being squandered as government power rises.

Gold is the natural enemy of socialism. There is no good reason why Americans cannot be fully protected by gold against socialism—the most dangerous threat to their life, liberty, and property.

18

HOW TO RETURN TO THE GOLD STANDARD

A return to the gold standard is crucial to Americans. Waiting for the current fiat system to collapse is neither responsible nor ethical. Any attempt at restoring monetary freedom must be part of a comprehensive plan to roll back government within the limits of the Constitution. The gold standard is the only protection an individual has against economic and political tyranny—inflation, taxation, and confiscation.

The value of our dollar, under the current monetary system, is determined not by the amount of gold or the amount of goods produced, but by the politicians in power who have corrupted our money. The arbitrary power to issue debt currency must be stopped. The best method is through the reestablishment of the gold standard. The following suggestions come from two sources: Alden Rice Wells' article, "Spending Money,"[1] which together with its supporting materials was sponsored for a Nobel Prize in Economics. The second is Ron Paul's "The Case for Gold," which is produced from the 1982 Gold Commission. The plan is designed to eliminate the instabilities of the present monetary system and to restore value to money.

Claims have been made that the gold in Fort Knox is gone, perhaps since 1971. The government hasn't tried to disprove that claim with an audit. However, according to a CNN article on 11/12/2009, "The Treasury Department has 261.5 million ounces of gold in its reserves." Either way, if the gold is gone or it exists, the suggestions below will take that into account.

Since economic order breeds political order, time is of the essence. Honest spending money is the vital element in domestic tranquility. As government has taken it upon itself to furnish the country with a medium of exchange, it is required by the Constitution to furnish gold and silver. Since government is the sole issuer and regulator of the money supply, it does no good for it to blame the declining purchasing power on others.

It is not enough to permit citizens to own gold while forcing them to use only government paper money as legal tender. In order to stop currency depreciation, citizens must have the right to refuse the use of government money and the right to choose any commodity they wish to use. Monetary freedom ends where legal tender laws begin.

The first step toward sound money is to remove *all* restrictions on buying, selling, owning, and trading gold from American citizens. United States citizens must be allowed to own gold in the United States or anywhere else in the world, *in any* form they wish and without any discriminatory tax. To insure this all-important step, the legal tender laws must be repealed. In 1862, Congress forced acceptance of Lincoln greenbacks as a wartime emergency. That "emergency" has lasted 147 years; it is time that this unconstitutional action by Congress is repealed. This would free Americans from monetary bondage and give back to them their Constitutional right.

Assuming the government still has a gold reserve, a second major reform is a legal definition of the term "dollar." The Gold Commission of 1982 suggested "defining a 'dollar' as a weight of gold of certain fineness, .999 fine." It also recommended a new gold coinage. They should be struck in one ounce, one-half ounce, one-quarter ounce, and one-tenth ounce weights, using the beautiful Saint Gaudens design in 1907. Americans must be allowed to exchange their paper money for genuine American coins—no need to buy foreign gold coins. All forms of taxes—capital gains, excise and sales—be removed so the new coinage can quickly become an alternative monetary system to the present paper monopoly.

Independent of government, private mints should also be allowed to issue their own coins under their own trademarks and be protected by law. In fact, all foreign currencies, private coins, government coins, private bank notes, and so on should trade freely, permitting the public to choose the most reliable currencies, and allowing the less reliable to be displaced.

It is imperative that the United States government and all institutions dependent upon it, including the Treasury, keep entirely out of the gold market. A *free* gold market cannot come into existence if the government were to try to manipulate the price by underselling, or by imposing a discouraging tax. The new monetary system must be protected against malicious acts by officials of the Treasury.

Third, all Federal Reserve Notes are turned over to the Treasury and are replaced by U.S. non-interest bearing notes, thus eliminating the debt and interest to note holders. This may take a year or two. At the same time, the Federal Reserve System is abolished. The necessity of this is apparent. In 1946, the income of the Fed was $104 million. In 1973 it was 3.8 billion. In 2008 the Fed's net income was $21 billion. Here is a vested interest, a private corporation that has expanded its power unequaled by any other bureaucracy. It would also end a power-hungry private corporation.

Gold money and government money would circulate side by side preventing a severe deflation in the money supply, wages, and prices. Gold could be deposited in a bank for a receipt. Competition would also strengthen government money by breaking up the monopoly government holds. It would be unable to further inflate the money supply to finance wars, welfare programs, bail outs, etc. Balancing the federal budget would now be required and made possible by a debt-free monetary system.

Fourth, withdrawal from foreign organizations dangerous to U.S. interests: International Monetary Fund (IMF), Bank of International Settlements (BIS), and the World Bank. (The United Nations would probably qualify here too.)

Fifth is abolishing the fractional reserve banking system, which has created 90 percent of our inflation. Banks ought to be free and independent of government manipulation. Banking reform would mean all promises to pay on demand, whether made in notes or deposits, be backed 100 percent by whatever is promised, gold, silver or cantaloupes. Any failure to do so would be subject to severe penalties. Competition in the banking industry would break up the trend toward fewer and bigger banks. Freely traded gold coins would give consumers an alternative to bank notes and government notes.

If the government wished to mint gold and silver coins of good quality it could do so. The profit it receives from "making money" would be sharply reduced. For example, not long ago a silver quarter cost the government about twenty cents. Today its replacement, the base metal quarter, costs less than two cents. A one thousand dollar note cost pennies and the government can buy one thousand dollars worth of goods with it. This profit, or seigniorage, is the easiest method governments extract money from the people without it being noticed. The additional cost of gold and silver money would reduce the government's seigniorage substantially. The added value would be passed on to the people. Gold coins would again be in the cash holdings of the people, along with government money and checkbook money.

Sixth, there are at least three other powerful departments intent on building their own bureaucracies: the Treasury Department, the Office of Management and Budget, and the Council of Economic Advisors. The Constitution designated the Secretary of the Treasury as the officer in charge. The other competing departments should be abolished.

The seventh step requires denouncing any attempts to keep the dollar's parity rate fixed by recreating parities either for gold or the dollar. A completely free gold market, where the dollar and gold are allowed to seek their own market levels, is the only way to stabilize the currency. Gold and other notes should also be accepted in payment of taxes.

Other steps needed are a complete and transparent audit of the gold reserves, if there are any, by the Treasury so it can be determined if the government can mint gold coins; repeal of the laws empowering the President to confiscate privately owned gold bullion, gold coins and gold certificates in time of war; repeal the 1864 law creating a banking monopoly; eliminating discriminatory treatment of gold coins in IRAs. Retirement accounts should be free to keep gold coins without incurring a penalty; repeal mining regulations that make it difficult and expensive to open and operate gold and silver mines. All regulations on the export, import, melting, mining, and hoarding of gold coins be repealed.

Rep. Paul's Gold Commission proposed a Constitutional amendment to reaffirm the right to gold:

Neither Congress nor any state shall make anything a tender in payment of private debts, nor shall they charter any bank or note-issuing institution, and states shall make only gold and silver coins as tender in payment of public taxes, duties, and dues (p. 185).

Government deficits and living beyond its means are not compatible with the gold standard and economic freedom. Following W.W. II, President Truman massively cut spending and taxes. Over a three year period, 75 percent of the federal budget was eliminated. It can be done!

It is time the United States put its house in order. Both reason and experience prove that the gold standard contributes to a greater stability in prices than exists under any other monetary standard. F. A. Hayek points out that in the United States, during the period 1749-1939 (see previous chart), there does not seem to have occurred a significant upward trend of prices. Compared to the rate at which prices have risen during the last half century (during the dollar standard), there has been a significant rise in prices.

Purchasing Power of Gold
(1792 = 1.00)

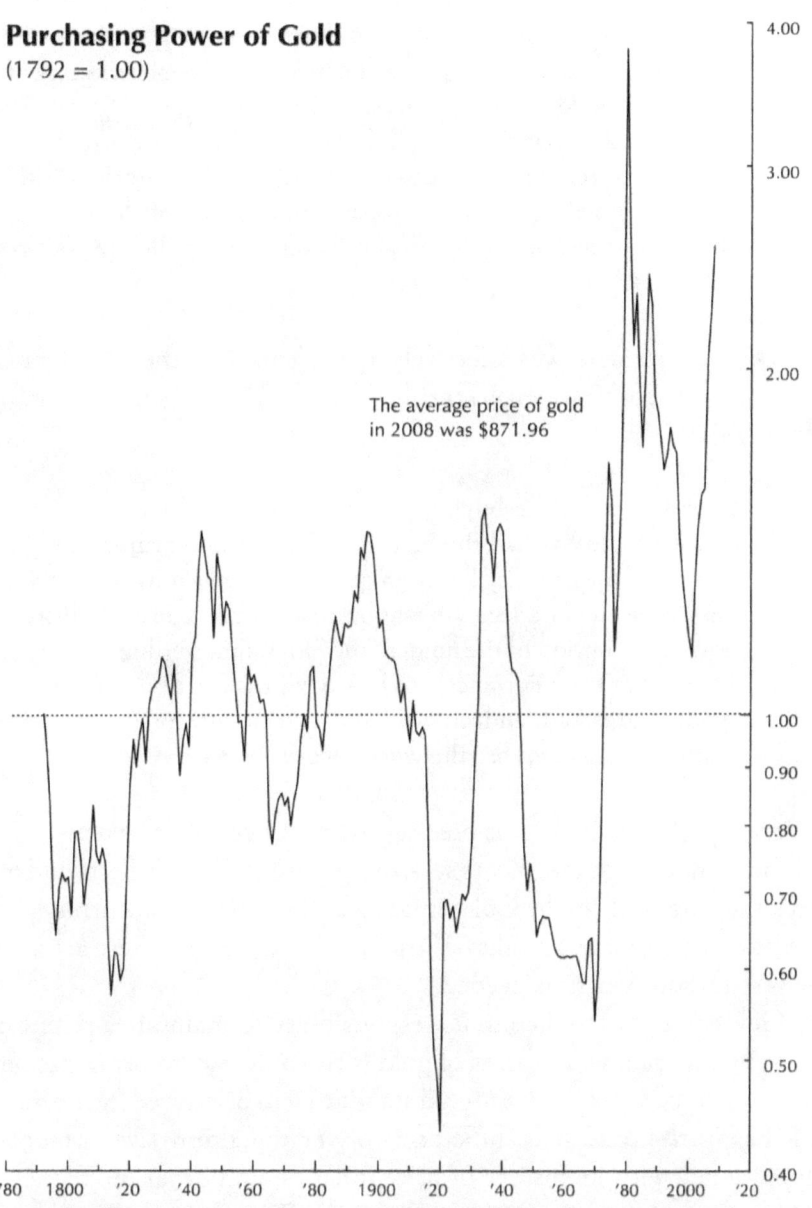

The average price of gold
in 2008 was $871.96

Note: The changes in purchasing power shown in the chart were calculated from annual averages of the Wholesale Price Index (source: Bureau of Labor Statistics, U.S. Department of Labor) and the annual averages of the exchange ratio of dollars for gold.

To what extent the record can be described as one of "creeping inflation" or "chronic inflation" or "galloping inflation" or whatever, is somewhat beside the point. Since abandoning the traditional gold standard, the record certainly does not point to any appreciable deflationary influences in the long-run view. The upward movement of prices during the 20th century contrasts sharply with the period of effective functioning of the gold coin standard in the United States and Britain during the previous two centuries?[2]

The case for gold was effectively summarized by the National City Bank of New York in their Monthly Letter of December, 1951, on page 135:

Fluctuations in the buying power of money are familiar over all history. Gold has had the best record over the centuries as a store of value. Paper money has been good when issued by banks which have been under a legal obligation to maintain convertibility into gold at the option of the holder. The old pound sterling and the old U.S. dollar were currencies of this type; their very names become synonymous with enduring value. Paper money directly issued by National Treasuries has the worst record. . . .[3]

Henry Hazlitt said, "It is precisely when a free gold market is needed that most modern governments seek to suppress it. For it reflects and measures the extent of the lack of confidence in the domestic currency; and it exposes the fictitious quality of the 'official' rate. And these are among the very reasons why it is needed."[4]

Government has failed in its responsibility to maintain a strong currency. Freely trading all forms of gold is the only way to bring back economic stability. Over time, the gold standard will be created by the market as it has in the past. It is difficult to prefer the alternative of managed paper money with its history of price inflation and deflation, money depreciation, and loss of individual freedoms. The gold standard has run into trouble only when governments interfere with its operations. An automatic monetary mechanism such as the gold standard is decidedly superior to arbitrary monetary powers in promoting economic stability.

The question of the gold standard versus the paper standard will be solved soon—either under the pressure of emergency or with quiet thoughtful deliberation. To wait for the emergency is to invite disaster. To spare the American people the disorder and suffering of a crisis of cataclysmic proportions, the proper action must be taken now.

The closing of the gold window in 1971 was an admittance of government's insolvency. The United States government must start protecting its citizens. There is no better way than by encourage them to freely own and trade gold and silver.

History shows us how crises have led to a larger federal government and greater centralization. Today's crisis is being used to nationalize large private corporations, bail out friends of the Fed, and grab more power in general. President Obama's chief of staff, Rahm Emanuel, said, "You never want a serious crisis to go to waste." The President concurred.[5] We are so used to government intervention that we think that the only way government can be the protector of last resort is through the sacrifice of personal liberty. We are already over-regulated. The only regulations missing are the ones on government officials and the Fed who are running roughshod over the people, their money and the Constitution.

When gold and silver are traded freely, the gold standard will reestablished itself, either with or without Treasury gold. The future will be secure from the tyranny of devastating inflations, depressions and despotic government. It is time to make the government respect our rights and private property. To stop inflation, demand gold and end the Fed and our debt based monetary system. All Americans can and must unite on this stand.

19

GOLD GOES WITH FREEDOM

Down through the ages, the history of man has been one of tyranny and oppression. The periods of freedom during ancient Greece and Rome were brief. Freedom has been the exception. The true revolution for human freedom, the revolution of ideas, was the only new and glorious change that happened to the race of man in over 6,000 years of history. The founding of the United States of America was where man finally created the reality of individual freedom.

The degree of any country's freedom determines the exact degree of its progress. America, the freest country, achieved the most. Americans owe their high standard of living to the economic system, which presupposes individual freedom and property rights —Capitalism.

Capitalism leaves every man free to choose the work he likes, to specialize in it, to trade his product for the product of others, and to, go as far on the road of achievement as his ability and ambition will carry him. The basic premise of the Founding Fathers was man's right to his own life, to his own liberty, and to the pursuit of his own happiness. The political implementation of this right is a society where men deal with one another as traders, by voluntary exchange, for mutual benefit. To guarantee freedom to one individual requires that freedom be guaranteed to all individuals. Capitalism implements this guarantee.

The opposite of freedom is slavery. Socialism implements slavery through government planning, regulations, taxation and inflation. The experience of recent decades has shown that government-created inflation via the Fed has been confiscating individual wealth as it increases the size and reach of government. As this process continues, individual liberty will eventually be abolished in favor of government control. The people will get what they are asking for—security instead of freedom.

The contrast between the two systems is clear. The central bank, the Fed, is refusing to allow past inflation to deflate and liquidate debt. Through its lies, deception and brainwashing, the Fed is doing everything possible to prevent capitalism from finding equilibrium. It is prolonging the meltdown and using the meltdown to bail out friends and grab more power.

The free price mechanism can achieve in hours what socialist, central bank, and planning—although reinforced with dictatorial powers—will always fail to achieve, no matter how many years it tries. The free price system allows profit and, as David Ricardo rightfully said, "Nothing contributes so much to the prosperity and happiness of a country as high profits."

To want freedom without wanting the conditions that make it possible is to ask to be keenly disappointed. To repeat Franklin, "They that can give up essential liberty to obtain a little temporary safety, deserve neither liberty nor safety." Individual freedom is the surest way to peace and prosperity. To implement the capitalistic society, a sound monetary system must exist. Sound money is truly the only road to a free and prosperous country.

Money, which is necessary to insure the peaceful and profitable exchange of goods and services and the fulfillment of contracts, must be a unit of exchange of the highest quality and of universal validity. That means gold. Wherever gold has been permitted to perform its function as only a unit of gold convertibility can, it has insured economic stability, pride and a sense of security among the people, giving strength to the character of the nation itself. Gold embodies the element of integrity, without which no nation can lay just claim to leadership or true greatness.

Historically, the record of man's outstanding successes has been written when the monetary supremacy of gold was recognized and encouraged, and his most colossal failures have resulted from trying to manufacture the illusion of wealth from the promises and threats of government.

In his often quoted, but always appropriate piece of advice, George Bernard Shaw summarized the importance of money and of gold:

> The most important thing about money is to maintain its stability so that a dollar will buy as much a year hence, or ten years hence, or fifty years hence as today, and no less. With paper money this stability has to be maintained by the Government. With a gold currency it tends to maintain itself even when the natural supply of gold is increased by the discovery of new deposits, because of the curious fact that the demand for gold in the world is practically infinite. You have to choose (as a voter) between trusting to the

natural stability of gold, and the natural stability, and the honesty and intelligence of the members of the Government. And, with due respect to those gentlemen, I advise you, as long as the Capitalistic system lasts, to vote for gold.

Not heeding Shaw's advice, the United States abandoned the gold standard in favor of a central bank. To support the Fed, Congress has increased the debt limit 90 times since 1940 (OMB). The planned economy has suffered from two world wars, many "conflicts," and endless inflation. It has witnessed the moral decline of its citizenry. This is the shabby secret of the welfare-statists-socialists' tirades against gold: inflation is simply a nefarious scheme for the "hidden" confiscation of wealth, which enriches bankers and pays for wars. Gold stands in the way of this insidious process. It stands as a protector of property rights and of life itself. It keeps the moral fiber of a country as strong and self-reliant as its money.

Mises warned that the struggle against gold must not be looked upon as an isolated phenomenon. It is but one item in the gigantic process of destruction which is the mark of our time. People fight the gold standard because they want to substitute national autarky for free trade, war for peace, totalitarian government omnipotence for liberty.[1]

This is socialism—war instead of peace, arbitrary government planning instead of individual freedom, promises instead of prosperity. Socialism is a coercive society. Trade is not done voluntarily, but under force. Reason is abandoned for the gun. Socialism is based upon fundamental fallacies and must, therefore, create social disintegration.

The gold standard is an integral part of capitalism. As such, the principles of the gold standard must be understood, or any freedom to own gold would result in economic chaos, for which the gold standard would be blamed. And all privately owned gold would again be confiscated and the gold issue defeated.

The gold standard is simple to understand. It is a hard-money standard, which cannot be printed or otherwise manipulated by politicians. It frees the individual holder from swindling and expropriations by the politicians. It keeps politicians honest. It is an essential safeguard for the preservation of the value of the currency and of human liberty.

Gold is the noblest of all metals. It is precious. Since it is almost indestructible, it has become a symbol of life. Gold in ancient times was equated with human life because it was used as a standard to measure the value of other things. And since it could be trusted to maintain its own worth, it was accepted in place of life itself. In fact, a gold ring was part of the price of buying a wife.

In modern times gold came to the rescue of American fliers that were forced down in the North African desert. In 1943, rewards of $1,000 gold were offered and paid for the assistance and safe return of American fliers.

The *New York Times* on July 16, 1967, printed the news that in 1967 American planes dropped millions of gold-colored leaflets over North Vietnam; they were captioned: "Reward—Fifty Taels of Gold—Reward." It explained that anyone helping a downed American flier escape could obtain this reward, about $1,760 in gold bullion.

Gold money is the money of last resort. It is universally accepted. It is no accident that so many gold coins have survived from ancient times, or that gold coins of modern history can be found so frequently in brilliant uncirculated condition. It is the nature of the metal itself, as well as man's nature to desire to possess something of enduring value, that provides the answer. Gold is the key to confidence, honesty and integrity.

The essential principles of sound money are impregnable. Keynes warned that to destroy a country one had only to "debauch the currency." Since 1934, the Americans have been fighting gallantly to survive monetary despotism. If you wonder why the quality of workmanship has deteriorated, job security is an issue, high unemployment exists, retirement funds have lost value, people are confused and worried, take a good look at the value of the nation's currency. The nation is being ravaged economically and morally by inflation.

The gold standard's time has come. It is the American way. It represents honesty and integrity. Throughout our history the battle has raged between hard money and paper money. Hard money won in 1787, in 1832, and in 1900; it can win again. The gold standard and ending the Fed can stop inflation. Eventually, the future of the dollar and of the country will be decided by those who control the world's gold.

Thomas Jefferson observed that mankind is disposed to suffer while evils are sufferable. Inflation is no longer sufferable. Fight for the gold standard as a moral issue. Many corporations have lost their moral compass. (Big "Pharma" has been "granted" immunity from liability for flu vaccine, www.Mercola.com,8/20/09.) Corporations are going begging to

Washington to be bailed out with our money. Industries are being nation-alized. On July 16, 2009, the American Medical Association endorsed House legislation to establish government medicine. Industry giants are selling their souls, capitalism and liberty wholesale. Only the open and unrestricted support of capitalism, abolishing the Fed and the fractional reserve system, and the gold standard can prevent America from enslave-ment by the barbarians of socialism that run the government.

The time has come, said Governor Morris, one of the Founding Fa-thers speaking of the Constitution, ". . . to raise a standard to which the wise and honest can repair . . ." Today the gold standard needs to be raised because Americans still suffer evils.

It is no accident that the 19th century is known as the century of peace and the gold standard. It is no accident that the 20th century since the creation of the Fed in 1913, is termed the century of inflation and wars. Today, the Fed deals secretly with trillions of dollars and refuses to open its books to Congress. Recently, when Elizabeth Coleman, Inspec-tor General of the Fed was asked where the $9 trillion worth of credit was extended in the past 8 months has gone, she replied that she had no idea. That's $30,000 for every man, woman and child in the U.S.! Rep. Paul has introduced the Federal Reserve Transparency Act, HR 1207. The Fed has stonewalled Congress for decades. Congress will act when citizens demand it. (To understand how the Fed was secretly formed, read "End the Fed".)

Everyone who works, saves, invests, or is retired, has a vested inter-est in the gold issue. Your voice is a powerful weapon. Politicians must pay attention when *We the People* demand ending the Fed and relying on the Constitution. Government's responsibility is to protect the domestic tranquility, i.e., economic and political stability, and drastically reduce the possibility of war. The U.S. is at a political and philosophical crossroad. Either we return to the Constitution, to the gold standard, or we continue down the path of least resistance and enter a coercive society. Liberty is compromised with each new welfare program and with every new war financed by fiat money.

As an illustration of the difference between the two types of societies compare the following quotes:

> The power of coining money and of regulating its value was delegated to Congress by the Constitution for the very purpose, as assigned by the framers of that instrument, of creating and

preserving the *uniformity* and *purity* of such a standard of value.— UNANIMOUS opinion of the U.S. Supreme Court in 1850. [Italics mine]

Gold is not necessary. I have no interest in gold. We'll build a solid state, without an ounce of gold behind it. Anyone who sells above the set prices let him be marched off to a concentration camp! That's the bastion of money. Adolf Hitler.[2]

It is shocking to see how far down the path of dictatorship we have come. On December 16, 2008 President Bush said on CNN: "I have abandoned free-market principles to save the free-market system."[3] This is the same reasoning they used to justify killing civilians in Vietnam. Government is corrupt and destructive.

Jacob Bronowski, in the end of his book *The Ascent of Man*, warned that "knowledge is not a loose-leaf notebook of facts. Above all, it is a responsibility for the integrity of what we are, primarily of what we are as ethical creatures. You cannot possibly maintain that informed integrity if you let other people run the world for you while you yourself continue to live out of a ragbag of morals that come from past beliefs."

The road to economic health begins by ending the Fed and recognizing gold. Economist John Maynard Keynes quoted Lenin as declaring the best way to destroy the capitalist system was to debauch the currency. We need to regulate the regulators, i.e. Congress, the Treasury and the Fed. That's what the gold standard can do. Inflation is crushing the United States. To survive inflation as a free nation, we must reform the entire monetary system.

Americans are banding together for freedom. Groups are marching on Washington or protesting in Chicago, demanding accountability from elected officials. There's a lot of public unrest and support for Ron Paul's bills. "...when a long train of abuses and usurpations...evinces a design to reduce them under absolute despotism, it is their right, it is their duty, to throw off such government and to provide new guards for their future security." We either hang together, as Franklin warned, or we hang apart. This is the beginning of the second American Revolution.

To follow the Revolution go to www.campaignforliberty.com . Idaho has passed the Idaho Silver Legal Tender Resolution. Also, check out the

Sovereignty Proposal Movement at www.johnseilersblogs.com and medical doctors at www.takebackmedicine.org.

Today, as in the past, a sound monetary system is the condition of man's freedom and the key to his life, liberty and pursuit of happiness. Let's try FREEDOM for a change!

SELECTED BIBLIOGRAPHY

www.aier.org
www.campaignforliberty.com
www.cato.org
www.articles.mercola.com
www.fee.org
www.healthfreedomalliance.org
www.johnseilersblogs.com
www.mises.org
www.takebackmedicine.org

The Declaration of Independence

The Constitution of the United States of America

Allen, Gina, *Gold!*, New York: Thomas Y. Crowell Co., 1964.

Hazlitt, Henry, *Economics in One Lesson*, New York: Harper & Row, Publishers, 1946.
, *Man Vs. The Welfare State*, New York: Arlington House, 1969.
, *What You Should Know About Inflation*, 2nd edition, Princeton, New Jersey: D. Van Nostrand Company, 1965.

Paul, Ron, *End the Fed*, New York: Grand Central Publishing, 2009.
, *The Case for Gold*, Auburn, Alabama: The Ludwig Von Mises Institute, 2007.

Rand, Ayn, *Atlas Shrugged*, New York: The New American Library, 1957.
, *Capitalism: The Unknown Ideal*, New York: The New American Library, 1966.
, *The Virtue of Selfishness*, New York: The New American Library, 1964.

Rueff, Jacques, *The Age of Inflation*, translated by A. H. Meeus & F. G. Clarke, Chicago: Henry Regnery Co., 1964.

Rothbard, Murray N., *Depressions: Their Cause and Cure*, Lansing, Michigan: Constitutional Alliance, Inc.

Sennholz, Hans F., *Inflation or Gold Standard?*, Lansing, Michigan: Constitutional Alliance, Inc.

Von Mises, Ludwig, *Human Action: A Treatise on Economics*, 3rd edition, Chicago: Henry Regnery Company, 1963.
Planned Chaos, Irvington-on-Hudson, New York: The Foundation for Economic Education, 1947.
Planning for Freedom, 2nd edition, South Holland, Illinois: Libertarian Press, 1962.
The Theory of Money & Credit, new edition, Translated by H. E. Batson, Irvington-on-Hudson, New York: The Foundation for Economic Education, Inc., 1971.

END NOTES

Chapter 1
1. "The Price They Paid," a speech given at Independence Hall, Knott's Berry Farm, Buena Park, California, 1972.

Chapter 2
1. Clinton Rossiter, *1787 The Grand Convention* (New York: The Macmilian Co., 1966), pp. 61-63.

Chapter 3
1. Nathaniel Branden, *The Psychology of Self-Esteem* (Los Angeles: Nash Publishing Corp., 1969), p. 70.

Chapter 4
1. Theodore Macklin, "Short Changing Money," California Mining Journal (October, 1971), p. 9.

Chapter 5
1. Henry Hazlitt, *What You Should Know About Inflation* (New York: D. Van Nostrand Company, Inc., 1965), pp. 26-27. Reprinted by permission of Van Nostrand Reinhold Company.
2. Ludwig von Mises, *Human Action*: A Treatise on Economics (Chicago: Henry Regnery Company, 1963), p. 730.
3. Ibid., p.254.
4. Ibid., p.269.
5. Ibid, p. 775.
6. lbid., p. 620.

Chapter 6
1. Ludwig von Mises, *Planned Chaos* (New York: The Foundation for Economic Education, Inc., 1947), p. 75.
2. Ibid., pp. 23-24.
3. lbid., p. 48.

Chapter 7
1. Harry D. Schultz, *Panics and Crashes and How You Can Make Money Out of Them* (New York: Arlington House, 1972), p. 149.
2. Gary Allen, *None Dare Call It Conspiracy*, (California: Concord Press, 1971), pp. 43-45.

3. www.federalreserve.gov/releases/h41/Current/ and www.federal-reserve.gov/releases/h41/20080807/

4. Henry Hazlitt, *Economics in One Lesson* (New York: Harper & Row, Publishers, 1946), pp. 213-14.

5. Henry Hazlitt, *What You Should Know About Inflation*, p. 1.

6. Mises, *Human Action*, p. 412.

7. Henry Hazlitt, *Man Vs. the Welfare State* (New York: Arlington House, 1969), p. 215.

8. Mises, *Human Action*, pp. 470-71.

9. Donald I. Rogers, *How to Beat Inflation by Using It* (New York. Arlington House, 1970), p. 85.

10. Brian L Bex, *The Decline and Fall of the American Republic* (Indiana: The American Communications Network, 1971), pp. 31-32.

11. Henry Hazlitt, *The Failure of the New Economics* (New York: Van Nostrand Co., 1959), pp. 343-44.12

12. Hazlitt, *Man Vs. The Welfare State*, pp. 215-16.

Chapter 8

1. Donald J. Hoppe, *How to Invest in Gold Coins* (New York: Arlington House, 1970), p. 58.

2. Ibid p. 203.

Chapter 9

1. C.H.V. Sutherland, *Gold: Its Beauty, Power and Allure*, p. 156.

2. Bex, p. ii.

3. Elgin Groseclose, *Money, Man and Morals* (New York: Christian Freedom Foundation, Inc., 1963), p. 8.

Chapter 10

1. Sutherland, *Gold: Its Beauty* p 156

2. Gina Allen, *Gold!*

3. Ibid, p. 155-56.

4. Ibid., p. 184.

Chapter 11

1. Clinton Rossiter, *1787 The Grand Convention*, p. 44.

2. Alexander Hamilton, John Jay, James Madison, *The Federalist* (New York: Random House, The Modern Library, n.d.), pp 290-91

Chapter 12

1. Mises, *Human Action*, p. 471.

2. Hans Sennholz, *Inflation or Gold Standard?* (Lansing, Michigan: Constitutional Alliance,Inc., n.d.), pp. 6-7.

Chapter 13

1. Alan Greenspan, "Gold and Economic Freedom," *Capitalism: The Unknown Ideal* (New York: The New American Library, 1962). © Copyright 1966 by The Objectivist, Inc., pp. 89, 91-95. Reprinted by permission.

2. Jacques Rueff, *The Age of Inflation*, trans. by A. H. Meeus and F. G. Clarke (Chicago: Henry Regnery Company, 1964), pp. 7-8.

3. Ibid., pp. 40-42.

Chapter 15

1. American Institute Counselors, Inc., in their *Investment Bulletin*, April 17, 1972.

2. Newell H. Leppert, *Gold: The Natural Enemy of Socialism* (California: California Mining Journal, n.d.).

3. Economic Research Corp., *Market Perspective*, June 7, 1972, V, 2, P. 3.

4. Reuff, *The Age of Inflation*, p. 69.

5. Ibid, p. 29

Chapter 16

1. *Schultz, Panics and Crashes*, p. 123.

2. Dr. Murray Rothbard, *Economic Depression: Causes & Cures* (Lansing, Michigan: Constitutional Alliance, Inc., n.d.), pp. 13-18.

3. Ibid., pp. 25-26.

4. Sennholz, *Inflation or Gold Standard?*, p. 18.

Chapter 17

1. Howard S. Katz, *Committee to Reestablish the Gold Standard*, **85** Fourth Avenue, Suite 6M, New York, New York, 10003.

2. Rueff, *The Age of Inflation*, p. 85.

3. Hoppe, *How to Invest in Gold Coins*, p. 55.

4. George Racey Jordan, *Gold Swindle: The Story of Our Dwindling Gold* (Los Angeles: The Bookmailer, Inc., 1959), p. 9

5. Leppert, *Gold: The Natural Enemy of Socialism*.

6. Ibid.

7. Ibid.

8. Donald J. Hoppe, *How to Invest in Gold Stocks and Avoid the Pitfalls* (New York: Arlington House, 1972), p. 184

Chapter 18

1. Alden R. Wells, *Alden R. Wells Quarterly*, Exeter, New Hampshire, October, 1972.

2. Arthur Kemp, *The Role of Gold* (Washington, D.C.: American Enterprise Institute for Public Policy Research, 1963), p. 35.

3. Ibid., p. 37.

4. Inflation, pp. 56-57.

5. Paul, p. 120.

Chapter 19

1. *Human Action*, p. 476.

2. Hoppe, *How to Invest in Gold Stocks*, p. 99, quoted from H. R. Trevor-Roper, *Hitler's Secret Conversations* (New York: Farrar-Straus, 1953), pp. 104-5.

3. Cited in *End the Fed*, p. 195

www.ingramcontent.com/pod-product-compliance
Lightning Source LLC
Chambersburg PA
CBHW032024170526

45157CB00002B/847